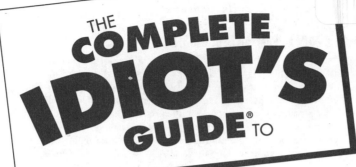

THE COMPLETE IDIOT'S GUIDE® TO

Wireless Computing and Networking

by Paul Heltzel

ALPHA

A Pearson Education Company

To Manhattan

Publisher: *Marie Butler-Knight*
Product Manager: *Phil Kitchel*
Managing Editor: *Jennifer Chisholm*
Acquisitions Editor: *Eric Heagy*
Development Editors: *Eric Heagy, Nancy D. Warner*
Senior Production Editor: *Christy Wagner*
Copy Editor: *Molly Schaller*
Illustrator: *Jody Schaeffer*
Cover/Book Designer: *Trina Wurst*
Indexer: *Tonya Heard*
Layout/Proofreading: *Svetlana Dominguez, Cheryl Lynch*

Contents at a Glance

Contents

Appendixes

Foreword

If you're like me, you leaf through a book to get a feel for what's in it. You probably think that the foreword and preface can provide some clues, and if I'm doing my job right, this one will. Here's what you'll find in this book:

- How to get the same mobility for your e-mail that your cell phone already provides for voice
- How to get stuff you care about from the Internet without all the ads and fluff you *don't* want
- How to connect and synch your Palm or Pocket PC PDA from anywhere
- How to figure out whether mobile computing might be useful to you
- How to pick out the best hardware, software, and network

This isn't just about mobility, however. A big part of this book is for people who don't need to stray too far from home or office. You'll be wanting to read this book if you need to figure out …

- How to get every computer in the house to share your cable modem connection.
- How to use that new color printer in the office without connecting your laptop to it.
- How to add a computer station for a new employee without first paying the electrician to drill holes in your walls and pull cable.
- How to answer every one of your boss's e-mails and get your assignment in on time, even though you—and your laptop—are enjoying a sunny day out on your deck.

All those things have one thing in common: operating a computer (or a data device of *some* sort) without having it connected to a phone jack or a network cable. If that's of interest to you, then this book is exactly what you're looking for.

Okay, Here's Where the Foreword *Really* Starts

I was flattered when I was asked to help with Paul Heltzel's book, *The Complete Idiot's Guide to Wireless Computing and Networking*. I was probably asked because I've been a part of the wireless computing industry since 1993, except it was called "wireless data" back then. I was still here when it re-dubbed "mobile computing," and then "wireless for the corporate user." In fact, I've lasted all the way through to the current name, "wireless Internet." I've served a number of jobs in that time: lecturer, consultant, trainer, author, journalist, and, by the time wireless Internet rolled around, I had worked myself up to being a full-time wireless industry analyst.

This is my first real foray into a publication for a mass audience, and I have wanted to say just one thing …

> WHERE HAVE YOU GUYS BEEN?! WE'VE SPENT <u>YEARS</u> GETTING WIRELESS INTERNET READY JUST FOR YOU! C'MON, LET'S GET GOING!! SIGN UP AND LOG ON FOR WIRELESS COMPUTING!

Okay, with that out of my system, here's what has gone into getting us to this point.

"This Isn't New, Is It?"

Through all those new names, we in the wireless computing industry have had a vision of the way the world could be. We wanted you to use your mobile phone to check on when your flight is arriving. We thought you should use your PDA to read your e-mail in a taxicab and even—like that famous TV commercial—use your computer to send a fax from the beach.

Every time somebody rolled out a new business plan, a new network, or a new wireless product of some sort, we watched in eager anticipation—then growing dismay—as new subscribers failed to materialize. We were always shocked that every grandmother, kindergartner, soccer mom, road warrior, and teenager hadn't actually started using wireless data communication.

So the wireless data users stayed away even at a time when cellular phone use was skyrocketing. Wireless networks carriers, software writers, content providers, and device manufacturers have been forced to examine and re-examine their products, trying to find the best combination to attract subscribers and bring wireless data communication into full bloom.

But we have been doing this for *years!* Have you seen those BlackBerry pagers that business travelers are using to tap out e-mails with their thumbs using that tiny keyboard? I saw the first one in 1996, and the network it uses has been running—and seeking new customers—since 1994.

So in many ways, the networks, devices, applications, and ideas for this mobile Internet—for wireless computing—aren't new at all. Many of the pieces have been in place for … well, a century, and have been undergoing constant improvement the whole time.

Why Wireless Computing Makes Sense

First a bit of history. Really, really old people—like me—remember the time when your home phone was the property of the Bell System and sat on a piece of furniture called a telephone table. The phone was usually in a hallway, and it had a cord about six feet long. Communication at that time was about being in a place.

The closest thing most people had come to a computer at that time was watching a documentary showing rooms full of hot vacuum tubes, flashing lights, and attentive technicians busily changing platter-sized tape reels.

It's safe to say that phones have changed a lot since then—and so have computers.

Wireless

Few inventions have made such a big impact in so few years as the mobile phone. The first cellular phone call was made in Chicago on a fall day in 1983. Only 15 years later (which, admittedly is two centuries in computer years), there were some countries that boasted over half their population using cell phones.

Since they really started to catch on in the mid-1990s, cellular phones have become smaller, lighter, and less expensive to purchase due to the economies of scale. The cost of using a mobile phone has plummeted as well. According to records kept by the Cellular Telephone and Internet Association, the average monthly cellular bill in 1990 was over $90. It declined to under $40 by 1998 and is now edging back upward as more people choose monthly plans with thousands of minutes and many are even replacing their home phone with their mobile.

It's pretty clear that that wireless communication is technologically well developed and that it has become an important part of our lives and a commonplace sight in our society.

Data

Data has become a big part of our lives as well. How long has it been since you have seen a typewriter or carbon paper? How about a vinyl LP record or an adding machine? An all-in-one product called the personal computer has replaced these items and many others. Not only is a large amount of our work and play in the form of data, we have also developed an excellent way to move it from one place to the other—that's using something called the Internet. As of 2001 in the United States, half the households have at least one personal computer. That's a mighty big number. North of the border, the numbers are even higher.

For example, I'm working at a desktop computer, and the Internet is so crucial to me that I use it nearly eight hours a day. And all of that crucial information comes to me from a cord that looks just like the six-foot cord that was on my grandmother's old rotary phone in the hallway. That's because it is!

Devices

Are you starting to see the pattern here? Lots of mobile phones, lots of people using data to communicate … what could possibly prevent anyone from getting at their data while mobile? The first thing that comes to my mind is the size of my computer. My desktop PC will definitely not be going to the beach, but my Palm-powered PDA or my smart mobile phone will. There are a surprising number of mobile phones, palm-sized computers, miniature laptops, and sub-notebooks, all of which display data from the Internet in one way or another and are small and light enough to tote in a shirt pocket, purse, or a backpack.

So the three pieces are in place. Widespread acceptance of mobile phones and their networks, the popularity of data communication, and computing devices small enough to carry. So what's left? The decided lack of *standards*.

Standards

The one thing that the old black rotary phone in the hallway had going for it was that it could connect to any other phone anywhere in the country (if you were willing to pay for long distance) or even any phone in the world, if you were willing to put up with the hassle. They worked on a common standard that connected two telephones from anywhere to anywhere and would (without fail) be added to your bill at the end of the month.

The wireless world, and the wireless data world in particular, was very guilty of not adhering to standards. As far as mobile communications in the Americas, standards are still evolving; they are much better throughout the rest of the world. Wireless office networks (called wireless local area networks or wireless LANs) are much more advanced. There has been a revolution in the industry that resulted from the acceptance of a standard that enables you to mix and match equipment from a variety of vendors. Paul discusses that standard, called Wi-Fi, in detail in this book.

So Where Are We Going?

Think of 1994 as the Stone Age of wireless computing. By the late 1990s we were in the Renaissance and are now in the Age of Enlightenment and maybe even up to the Truman administration.

The equivalent of the Space Age is right around the corner. The Internet, the World Wide Web, mobile phones, personal computers … all of this has happened in less than 10 years!

The advancements on the horizon for wireless are all about speed—speed for both mobile and in-home/in-office wireless local area networks.

Mobile Phones, Mobile Computing, and Third Generation Wireless

The shorthand for third generation wireless is "3G," and wireless will change dramatically once 3G is installed. Today's networks are barely capable of supporting download speeds of 14.4 thousand bits per second (or kbps). 3G networks are expected to offer users 384 kbps (that's 26 times faster than today) and maybe higher. Some 3G networks might even offer speeds rivaling DSL (the specification calls for 2,400kbps), although not for mobile users. The highest speeds, alas, will be reserved for users in fixed locations using modems that operate on household current and have large antennas mounted outdoors.

You can bet that widespread deployment of 3G networks will revolutionize mobile computing. The first networks are now in use in Asia; European and U.S. carriers are racing to offer 3G networks of their own. Today's second generation networks that display Internet information as text-only black-and-white handset screens will become more colorful, with graphics and images more like we are accustomed to seeing on our desktop computers. E-mail and text messages to your handset could have pictures attached, maybe snippets of music, or even simple animation or movie clips. You might even see weather radar images or color maps directing you to the nearest coffeehouse, pizza parlor, or gas station.

And when all that wireless network capacity isn't being used for graphics, music, video, or data, it will be used to increase the capacity for all the new subscribers who just want to call home at the end of a day at work.

Advanced Wireless Local Area Networks

When I accidentally end up in a room of network engineers—the ones who *loved* physics class and had a crush on their calculus teachers—I just try to figure out where the food is because I don't understand much of the conversation at all. The one thing that I *do* understand is that they are always tinkering with wireless technology and seem to be getting together and writing ambitious new standards with impossible specifications.

The Wi-Fi standard for wireless local area networks is one example. Wi-Fi, which the engineers call "802.11b," is capable of transmitting data at 11,000 kbps (just the first of a series of related standards). Upcoming versions are expected to run at least five times faster.

Why Start with Wireless Computing Now?

Over the years, the wireless data industry has made huge investments into research and development of networks, radio units, and applications that people will (and will not) want to use. It's like Thomas Edison as he labored to perfect the light bulb. When asked about thousands of "failures" to find the right material for a filament, Edison pointed out that he had actually succeeded, not failed, because he was closing in on the right answer by systematically eliminating the wrong answers.

It's the same with wireless computing (or wireless Internet or whatever we're calling it this week). All the necessary elements have been sorted out, many of the wrong answers have been eliminated, and now the wireless Internet is ready for you. The exciting innovations looming on the horizon will act to force prices of current-generation technology down and availability up for all the elements you'll need.

Don't let the promise of the coming high-speed networks prevent you from grabbing your share of wireless computing today. The cost of service is falling and equipment is becoming cheaper, faster, better, and more abundant. This really is the time to get started.

No matter how hard people in the wireless industry labor to make things work well, there is still the matter of finding out exactly what you need, what you already have, and how much you want to spend to accomplish your wireless computing goals. And Paul Heltzel's work in this book will do exactly that.

David Chamberlain
Kalamazoo, Michigan
2001

Introduction

Wireless technology isn't supposed to be hard to use. Apparently nobody told the people who make the stuff. There are conflicting standards, equipment that won't interoperate, and varying speed bumps you should avoid.

We can help you work your way through these hurdles and get straight to work, cord-free. If you read this book you'll learn about the two main ways of leaving wires behind:

> **Wireless Internet access**   Wireless phones, modems, and handheld Net devices are all great ways to stay connected. Which device should you buy and what can you do with it? *The Complete Idiot's Guide to Wireless Computing and Networking* knows all, tells all.

> **Wireless networking**   Why run wires all over your house to share your computers? No reason, really. With inexpensive wireless networking you can copy files from one computer to another, share Internet access, and surf the Web from your porch. It's very cool and really easy to set up. Easier if you read this book, but that goes without saying. Right?

So who needs this book? Anybody who takes a business trip and wants to keep in touch with the family and, if there's time, your boss. You'll find out how to pick up e-mail, send faxes, and find Internet sites that can make your wireless life easier. If your computers aren't connected, the poor dears, you can also use this book. And, if you can't get wired broadband (fast) Internet access, we'll look at satellite and other means of connecting quickly to the Net.

Along the way to wireless wisdom, we won't waste your time breathlessly enthusiastic toutings of the technologies. Instead, we'll look at the best technologies available, and even tell you if wireless isn't the best way to go.

Ready to unplug? Then let's get to work, and have some fun along the way. After all, wireless is supposed to make your life easier and let you get out of the office every now and then.

Special Reminders

As you read this book, watch out for these special features that will enhance your life and enrich your consciousness:

Bet You Didn't Know

Facts and figures about unplugging that you might find hard to believe.

Well-Connected Words

These sidebars turn the alphabet soup of wireless acronyms and jargon into terms you can use.

Watch Out!

Potential wireless snags you can avoid with a little extra information.

Synch Up

Tips and tricks for wirelessly connecting to the Internet and home-office networks. This feature takes its name from the process of connecting your PDA and computer to make identical the information you often need on them, such as your e-mail and schedule.

Acknowledgments

Thanks especially to Eric Heagy for all his help turning a proposal into the book you're holding now. Thumbs up to Dave Chamberlain for his technical editing and sharp eye for detail. Much appreciation to Nancy Warner, Christy Wagner, and Molly Schaller for pulling the manuscript into a sharp-looking book, and for thoughtful and concise edits.

Thanks to Neil Salkind at Studio B for continuing to help me find good writing projects, and to Stacey Barone for helping me make the rent on time. A high-five to my brothers for providing me with great office space to write. Of course, thanks to my wife, Deborah, without whose ideas and editing, this book would still be on a laptop somewhere in Tulsa. Finally, dear reader, thanks to you. If you happen to see a 1969 Airstream with a big antenna on top, anywhere in the campgrounds of America, stop by for a cup of coffee and some wireless chat.

Special Thanks to the Technical Reviewer

The Complete Idiot's Guide to Wireless Computing and Networking was reviewed by Dave Chamberlain, an expert who double-checked the accuracy of what you'll learn here, to help us ensure that this book gets all its facts straight.

David E. Chamberlain is Research Director of Probe's *Wireless Internet Services* Subscription Service. He recently completed two years as co-director of Probe's U.S. Competitive Service Markets Subscription Service and has extensive experience in both wired and wireless networks. His seminal study, *Wireless Data Networks: A Guide to Mobile Computing*, was first published in 1995 for The Bishop Company and remains in worldwide distribution. He has completed similar studies for the National Association of Broadcasters and has conducted extensive research studies for DoCoMo as well. A frequent speaker, his credits include the CDPD Forum (1997, general meeting), Motorola (1999) and Nortel (2000). He also plays a large role in Probe's ongoing coverage of FCC spectrum auctions, 3G technology/deployment, and fixed wireless systems.

Trademarks

All terms mentioned in this book that are known to be or are suspected of being trademarks or service marks have been appropriately capitalized. Alpha Books and Pearson Education, Inc., cannot attest to the accuracy of this information. Use of a term in this book should not be regarded as affecting the validity of any trademark or service mark.

Part 1

The Web Without Wires

Do you have places to go and people to see? Do you want to be able to move around with your data? Perhaps you want to work from exotic and remote locations like the Caribbean, the Arctic, or even your own backyard. But you want all the convenience and speed of a traditional wired office. We can help you with that.

First, we'll take a look at the wireless computing wonders available to you and which ones will best suit your needs. We'll run down some basic considerations as you create your plan and give you an idea of what your wireless setup will cost in time and expense.

In this first part, you'll get an overview of the technologies we'll discuss throughout the book, both fixed and mobile, and how they can work together.

Before You Disconnect: What Is Wireless Computing?

In This Chapter

- ◆ What is wireless computing?
- ◆ Your new wireless pals, all (soon to be) half a billion of them
- ◆ Finding the right device
- ◆ Ten ways to make wireless technology benefit you

If you can take your TV from one room to another, shouldn't you be able to browse the Internet from any room in your house or any coffee shop in town? With wireless technology—and some tips from this book—you can.

Hitting the road? With Internet-capable computing devices, such as a laptop or *PDA* connected to a modem, or access devices with built-in connections, such as a two-way pager or *smart phone* (sometimes called a Web phone) you can take the Internet with you, just about anywhere you go. At home or the office, you might want a wireless Internet connection so you can speed across the Web from the kitchen (instead of the room where the cable company drilled a hole in the wall). Maybe you have several computers that all need to share a modem and printer, and you don't want the hassle of opening your computer, installing networking cards in each PC, and connecting them with cables.

No problem. This book can help you do all these jobs. In this chapter, we'll get to know the most common wireless technologies to use where you live or work, or when you're traveling, and see how to get the most from them.

What It Is: The Wide World of Wireless

Recently a friend asked me for some advice on buying a new laptop. In addition to a speedy portable computer, he wanted some sort of wireless setup.

It was pretty clear to me that my friend didn't have a specific wireless technology in mind, but the idea of working without cords appealed to him. The problem is that *wireless* is a very broad term. Adding to the confusion, wireless technologies are many, and new ones are constantly being dreamed up by clever folks with computer science and engineering degrees.

For our purposes, we'll define wireless computing as those technologies that let us send and receive data, between two computers, without using cables. (Keep in mind these computers might be very small, and hidden inside a pager or cell phone.) In this book, we'll talk about cool wireless devices and technologies you can use today that make your life easier by keeping you connected and up-to-date without worrying about wires.

Wireless devices include pocket-size computers (specifically *Pocket PCs* and *Palms*), mobile phones, pagers, and laptop computers that can wirelessly send e-mail and browse the Web. Some of these devices, such as most PDAs, also can connect to laptop computers, and each other, using beams of light.

> **Well-Connected Words**
>
> **Smart phone** is a generic name for a mobile phone that can send and receive e-mail and instant messages, and browse the Web. A **PDA (Personal Digital Assistant)** is a handheld device used to manage e-mail, contacts, appointments, and sometimes access the Internet.

> **Well-Connected Words**
>
> A **Pocket PC** is Microsoft's name for handheld computers that run the Pocket PC operating system (or the OS formerly known as Windows CE, version 3.0).

You can also use modems that send and receive high-speed data, from anywhere that you can get a view of the southern sky, when you connect them to a satellite dish. Importantly, get these devices talking to each other, using wireless networks that enable you to share information between computers in your home or office.

Disconnecting: Why Go Wireless?

Beyond simply being a fun and useful technology, wireless computing is becoming hard to avoid. A recent study by Andersen Consulting reports that most American workers stay in touch with the office when they're on vacation. About 83 percent of those surveyed said they contact colleagues by e-mail and cell phone while they're on vacation. About 60 percent took some kind of mobile communications device along for the ride.

So clearly there's a desire to keep in touch when folks travel. And you don't even have to be a workaholic to use wireless technology. Even lazy writers like me want to find a good movie when I'm already on the run or get directions to a place I've never been. For those of us who appreciate a good acronym, you can use a wireless *WAN* (or *wide area network*) to get on the Internet on the road.

At home, the last things I need on my desk are more wires. The place is lousy with them. There I use a wireless *LAN* (or *local area network*) to connect my laptop, and my PDA, to the Internet.

Wireless networks, accessible at home and on the road are increasing in popularity, and soon, more people will access the Internet wirelessly than through traditional wired means, such as the services provided by your phone and cable company. Wireless is gaining in popularity for good reason: It keeps you in touch.

Well-Connected Words

A **LAN** (**local area network**) is a group of connected computers. A wireless, or wired, LAN allows you to share data, including Internet access, among all connected computers. A wireless **WAN** (**wide area network**) provides network (primarily Internet) access over a large geographic region.

Bet You Didn't Know

If you use the Internet wirelessly, you're not alone. Of the *one billion* people expected to use mobile phones by 2003, according to research firm The Yankee Group, 60 percent of those will be able to access the Internet wirelessly.

Stationary and Mobile Wireless Devices

When most people say wireless computing, they're talking about mobile access to the Internet. For instance, you might send e-mail, check stock quotes, or get sports scores using a mobile phone or PDA that runs software called a "minibrowser." We'll consider these devices' ability to handle other jobs as well, such as schedule management, but all the technologies and electronics covered will at least send e-mail without wires.

Well-Connected Words

A BlackBerry handheld is a wireless paging device from Research In Motion (RIM). Black-Berry handhelds and other two-way pagers send and receive e-mails. You can also use a BlackBerry to send a fax or access Microsoft Outlook or Lotus Notes servers. **Palm OS** is the operating system used by Palm handhelds.

Now it's time for an important distinction: Wireless devices come in many flavors, and not all of them fit in your pocket. We'll also check out stationary wireless devices that can help you get your work done faster.

Mobile wireless devices include the following:

- "Smart phones" such as those sold by Sprint PCS, AT&T, Voicestream, Cingular, and Verizon.
- Pocket PCs that use a Microsoft operating system (OS) that resembles the Windows OS.
- Palm devices, such as the Handspring Visor, that use the *Palm OS*.
- Two-way pagers, like the Motorola Talkabout (see Figure 1.1) and the *BlackBerry handheld*, a wireless paging device from a company called Research In Motion (RIM). BlackBerry handhelds and pager-sized devices send and receive e-mails. You can also use a BlackBerry handheld to send a fax.

Figure 1.1

Motorola's Talkabout T900 two-way pager.

In addition to these handy travel companions, wireless computing also includes the following stationary wireless devices:

- Satellite broadband modems for very fast Internet access. DirectPC and Starband (see Figure 1.2) are the two biggest consumer satellite broadband providers.

- Wireless networks that transmit data using radio waves in a home or office to connect computers and enable them all access to the same information (and the Web).

- Fixed wireless Internet access, a technology available in limited areas, provides fast Internet speeds through an antenna at that must have a straight shot through the air to the Internet access provider.

> **Synch Up**
>
> You can access the Internet using a wireless device, but you may not necessarily be surfing the Web. The Internet is an enormous network, providing access to all sorts of data, including some that's not on the World Wide Web, such as e-mail and instant messaging.

Figure 1.2

A Starband satellite dish makes its way to the University of Alaska. Fast Internet access is just a dog-sled ride away.

What Kind of Wireless User Are You?

Just about anybody can use wireless devices to get their work done more easily and quickly, but we'll concentrate on two main types of wireless folks—the business traveler and the home or office user.

The traveler depends on one or a handful of wireless devices to stay in touch with home or the office. These include PDAs with modems and two-way pagers that can send and receive e-mail, and have some capability for browsing the Web wirelessly. Travelers also usually depend on a laptop for e-mail (especially for sending attachments), Web browsing. The trick is keeping more than one computer synched up as you move around. We'll show you how to do that, in Part 3, "Wireless at Home and Work."

Bet You Didn't Know

Keep in mind that most handheld computers *do not* come with built-in wireless access. The Palm VII handheld is a notable exception, because this PDA comes with access to the Internet out of the box. In fact, it can get quite pricey to get your handheld on the Internet, because you'll need to purchase a modem and monthly wireless service. See the "Disconnect: Wireless Modems" and "Modems: Picking a Provider" sections in Chapter 9, "Ring Up the Web."

The wireless office user needs a way to keep handhelds and laptops current with the office network and with a personal computer. These tasks can be handled by sending information wirelessly. You transfer data from one device to another (say, from a PC to a PDA) or send information to a wireless network, which connects a number of wireless computers at home or at work.

Knowing what kind of user you are helps you create a plan for going wireless. That said, most people are a combination of both, and both stationary and mobile wireless devices can be of use.

After you know what you want to do with a wireless computer, it's much easier to figure out which devices are appropriate for you.

Leaving Cords Behind

Whether you need mobile or fixed wireless (or both) there are important benefits that aren't available to your unwired friends and colleagues. It's okay to feel a little superior. Go right ahead. Here's why.

With wireless devices you can …

♦ Reduce the paper you use by trading electronic versions of business cards.

♦ Stay in better touch with your kids and friends by using two-way e-mail devices that cost much less than a laptop computer.

♦ Hit the road without worrying about finding a phone jack where you can plug in your modem.

♦ Use one device that combines multiple functions (such as phone and e-mail) so that you can communicate more quickly.

♦ Forget about buying cables and fishing behind walls to create an office network.

> **Bet You Didn't Know**
>
> Fans at San Francisco 49ers football games are able to view stats and order food via handheld devices, which are connected wirelessly to vendors at the stadium. The devices are part of a wireless local area network and are loaned out for use during the game.

Ways to Make Wireless Work for You

All right, so we've talked about some of the general benefits of wireless technology. Still unconvinced that wireless is the best thing since sliced pepperoni? Well, here are more things you can do with the wireless skills you'll develop from reading this book:

♦ Forward your e-mail from your office account to your mobile phone

♦ Browse the Web from your favorite coffee shop

♦ *Beam* your schedule to your phone or PDA

♦ Collect a document you left back at the office

♦ Set up a simple wireless network so that you can take your laptop from your den to the back porch and maintain your connection to the Internet

- Update an appointment on your schedule and synch the change on your network so that your co-workers know you've moved the time
- Load your PDA with Web pages to read on a train to work, even if you can't get a connection to the Internet
- Get a review for and directions to a good restaurant on your next out-of-town business trip

- Use your phone to check the status of a flight
- Check your calendar wirelessly
- Set up fast Internet access by satellite at a home or office where folks can't get cable or DSL Internet service

Well-Connected Words

To **beam** is to send information from one device (such as a PDA) to another wirelessly, using infrared light.

Bet You Didn't Know

If you're used to the all-you-can e-mail pricing of your dial-up Internet account, you might be surprised by the cost of mobile messaging. Two-way pagers and e-mail capable "smart phones" often charge a fee per message, and sometimes include additional fees for messages over a certain length. Make sure to shop around for a provider that offers a pricing plan that includes messaging in the monthly fee and that it's appropriate for the amount of mail you plan to send and receive. Otherwise, you're likely to be shocked at the additional cost.

What to Do Now?

This book will help you learn about, shop for, and make good use of wireless computing devices. The next few chapters familiarize you with the technologies you need to know about. Because this area of technology changes to quickly, we'll help you do additional research and find answers on the Web.

In Chapter 2, "Avoiding Wireless Speed Bumps," we'll look at some situations where, despite all its charms, wireless technology can do more harm than good. And of course, we'll help you find ways around the hang-ups.

The Least You Need to Know

- ◆ Five hundred million people are expected to connect to the Internet using mobile devices by 2005 (according to a study by Allied Business Intelligence).

- ◆ Wireless is typically segmented into fixed and mobile. You can use fixed wireless for Internet access at home or the office and to network computers. Mobile wireless is typically for connecting PDAs, laptops, and smart phones to each other, desktop computers, the Internet, and networks while you're on the go.

- ◆ A wireless network enables you to share modems, printers, and the Internet from anywhere in your home or office.

- ◆ You can send e-mail wirelessly using a mobile phone, PDA, laptop, or two-way pager.

- ◆ Wireless broadband technologies offer connection speeds that meet and sometimes exceed those of their wired counterparts.

Avoiding Wireless Speed Bumps

In This Chapter

- ◆ Getting around limited coverage
- ◆ Wireless incompatibilities
- ◆ The future looks speedy
- ◆ Don't overlook wired options

Despite the promise of wireless technology, the reality is that going cord-free can lead to some sticky problems. Slow speeds, limited coverage areas, and incompatible networks are all areas where wireless computing could, as one's grumpy father might have said, "use a kick in the pants."

Because wireless computing is growing so quickly, there are competing, and sometimes incompatible, technologies to choose from. You have no lack of choices when you go shopping for wireless devices—the hard part is figuring out which one is right for you.

This chapter examines the drawbacks of using wireless technology. Of course, we won't leave you in a lurch. For each wireless speed bump, we consider the best available solutions. And, where wired technology makes more sense, we'll tell you that, too.

Bandwidth Blues

Most often, eager new wireless technology lacks speed when compared to more mature computing technologies that use wires.

So here we begin looking at bandwidth, or the speed at which your connection can transmit data (across an office network, for instance, or the Internet). The speed of a modem is usually measured in kilobits per second (kbps, or thousands of bits per second), and network connections are typically measured in megabits per second (mbps, or a million bits per second).

Although the modem that comes with your new laptop runs at 56kbps, you're lucky to get half that speed from wireless devices, such as the following:

◆ **Wireless modems.** Most wireless modem users access the Web on wireless networks that can supports speeds at no more than 14.4kbps. The modems slip into a laptop's PC Card slot or PDA expansion card slot (some, such as the Novatel Minstrel, also connect from the back of a PDA). Others connect to a serial port on the laptop or PDA. Access is sluggish, but you get just enough ooomph to read e-mail or browse text-based Web pages. Wireless modems from vendors including Novatel and OmniSky are available for laptops, Palm devices, and Pocket PCs.

◆ **Web Phones and PDAs.** Web phones (see Figure 2.1) and PDAs often access the Internet using *WAP* browsers. WAP stands for the Wireless Application Protocol, a standard for presenting text-based information on the Internet on handheld devices that don't have the computing firepower—or big screen—of your computer at home. Since speed is an issue, WAP browsers present the information you really need from the Web but leave the full-color graphics and advertisements behind.

Well-Connected Words

WAP (Wireless Application Protocol) is a standard for providing Internet access to smart phones and handheld computers. WAP allows these devices to pick up e-mail and browse low-fi Web pages, using a modified browser, usually called a mini-browser or microbrowser. WAP uses the Wireless Markup Language (WML), a modified version of HTML for small screens.

It's not always a bad trade. Sometimes you'll be able to access your information, like bank balances or a movie listing, more easily than you could by wading through standard Web pages. But activities such as shopping and research are tougher to manage using a slow connection and WAP browser.

Bet You Didn't Know

Because we often measure speed in kilobits (a thousand bits) or megabits (a million bits) per second, you might be wondering what a bit is. A bit, or binary digit, is the smallest amount of data a computer can store, a 0 or a 1. It takes eight bits to make a byte, which represents a letter, number, or symbol.

◆ **Wireless serial cable.** Some wireless travelers connect their laptops and PDAs to their existing cell phone using a special cable that usually sells for between $20 and $50. Most folks see a maximum speed of 14.4kbps using their mobile phone.

Figure 2.1

A Web phone allows you to check e-mail, check the Web, and send short text messages.

(Photo courtesy of Samsung)

◆ **Two-way pagers.** We've already discussed two-way pagers, and go into more detail in Chapter 10, "Wireless E-Mail Devices." Two-way pagers are handy for sending and receiving quick e-mails. You can't send attachments, though, which makes a laptop computer a better bet for working on files that need to be mailed back to the home office.

Sometimes Wireless Is Faster

Now, for the good news. The future of speeding along the Internet wirelessly is really promising, and wireless formats and devices just keep getting faster and faster.

In broadband wireless news, a promising technology called *GPRS* is beginning to appear from carriers, including AT&T Wireless, Cingular, and VoiceStream. GPRS, which stands for General Packet Radio Service, is a newer technology that offers quick surfing speeds and the ability to hold a conversation while surfing the Web. GPRS is expected to bump up Internet access speeds from 14.4kbps to 144kbps. Very promising, indeed.

In addition, a whole new generation of wireless technology is on the way. Called *3G*, for third generation, the technology allows mobile phone users to view streaming video, surf the Web at broadband speeds, and make voice calls from all over the world.

Well-Connected Words

GPRS (General Packet Radio Service) is a digital cellular phone standard, currently in limited use in metro areas, which can send and receive data at a speed between 56kbps and 114kbps. 3G, third generation wireless technology, is typically identified by one of three generations. The first generation, 1G, represented the analog voice communications of the 1970s and 1980s. In the 1990s, digital 2G communications were introduced and used primarily for voice and text messaging. We should see 3G in the next few years. The technology will provide faster transmission and global roaming capability. We might also use 3G technologies for high-quality, wireless audio and video transmission.

Getting Coverage Off the Beaten Path

Wireless e-mail and Web surfing can be incredibly useful business tools, until you get in a remote area. As soon as you leave the cosmopolitan ways of the Big City, it's hard to connect to your wireless network so that you can hop on the Internet.

If your budget allows, one way to increase your ability to get wireless Internet access is to use more than one service provider. For instance, choose one provider for your Internet-capable smart phone and one for your wireless modem.

Going with a laptop or PDA? If you purchase a wireless modem, you might sign up with a service that the modem manufacturer recommends. Or it might be less expensive to buy a second cell phone, from a different provider, and also purchase the serial cable that connects the phone to a laptop or PDA (sometimes this cable is referred to as a *connectivity kit*).

Obviously, using multiple accounts can get pretty pricey. I won't lie, I'm a penny pincher. But I like backups to my backups. If you're watching the bottom line, you can probably handle all your access needs through one national wireless network. A single-provider approach will save you on monthly fees, at the cost of some (useful) redundancy.

For wireless access at home or office in remote areas, the best (or perhaps only) current broadband option is fast, two-way satellite. Both StarBand (a partnership between Microsoft and EchoStar, the parent company of DISH Network), and Hughes Networks (which sells the DirectPC service) offer Internet access by satellite. Speeds are usually between 400 to 500kbps when downloading from the Internet, and 125 to 150kbps when uploading. The speed is expected to increase over the next few years as Net users become more bandwidth hungry, and bandwidth-hungry technologies like full-screen video become more common on the Internet.

> **CAUTION**
>
> **Watch Out!**
>
> Some wireless modems, especially those inserted into the PC Card slot of your laptop or PDA, can drain your computer's battery life. You might see as much as a 25 percent reduction in battery life when using a wireless modem. Many wireless modems are self-powered by a lithium-ion battery, but keep in mind that you'll need to keep them charged to stay connected.

Keep in mind that wireless Internet access is not for the mobile crowd. In fact, installing a satellite is most often a job for a professional technician, and the current providers do not support mobile access. Our sources tell us, however, that at least one of the satellite broadband companies is actively working on a mobile solution for folks with recreational vehicles, who are keenly interested in the technology as a fast, mobile means of Internet access.

Don't Overlook Cheaper Wired Options

When looking at wireless options, you might find that there are cheaper devices available that do a fine job for less money. Check out these cost cutters:

◆ **Dial-up modems.** Considering expense and accessibility, it's hard to beat a tried-and-true 56kbps modem. For sending and receiving e-mail and accessing the Web, a three-year-old modem still beats most wireless Internet access for speed and reliability.

◆ *Ethernet* **cables.** Wireless networks are increasing in popularity and becoming cheaper. Yet the cost of setting up a network with Ethernet cables (see Figure 2.2), the most popular type of network cabling, is considerably cheaper. Ethernet-based networks are especially attractive if connecting the computers by cables isn't too much trouble (or creates an eyesore). When creating a network, expect to pay about $20 per machine using Ethernet, as opposed to just under $100 per machine using wireless networking equipment. More on wireless networking expense and setup can be found in Chapters 3, "Unplug and Stay Connected," and 13, "Starting a Wireless Network."

Figure 2.2

Ethernet card and cable.

◆ **Pocketmail.** This $100 device for sending and receiving e-mail on the road is a handy companion to your wireless devices, especially when you're traveling to areas with spotty wireless mobile phone and pager coverage. Pocketmail connects to any phone—including a payphone—and lets you send e-mail messages up to 4,000 characters each (but no attachments).

Well-Connected Words

Ethernet is the most common type of wired network. The technology can reach a maximum data transfer speed of 100mbps and is used to share computers, printers, and Internet connections.

◆ **Laptops.** If your eyes say PDA, but your wallet says legal pad, consider holding on to your laptop, which can do all the same jobs—and more—and is just a bit bulkier. In the market for something new? Here wireless has the edge. Purchasing a new, or possibly even used laptop still can't compete, price-wise, with handheld organizers like the Handspring Visor ($149), Palm VII ($199), RIM Pager ($499), or Compaq iPAQ ($600).

Keep an eye out for auction sites with good deals on handheld computers. Palm devices are especially good bargains, because the Palm operating system has aged gracefully over the last few years and has most of the personal organizing features of newer models. The catch? PDA screens can be fragile and earlier models are more susceptible and are likely to have taken some abuse.

Trading Convenience for Speed

Convenience and freedom are the selling points of most wireless devices. When you decide to hit the road with a wireless modem—or sip tea in the backyard while surfing the Net—consider these tradeoffs:

◆ Although a 56kbps modem moves a 1MB file across the Internet in just under 2½ minutes, a 14.4kbps connection on a laptop connected to a wireless phone takes 7 minutes longer to do the same job and is less reliable because of dropped connections.

◆ An Ethernet-based local area network moves data across the network at 100mbps. A wireless network using 802.11b technology is still quite speedy, but considerably slower, at 11mbps.

◆ The Palm VII surfs the Web over a national wireless wide area network (WAN) at just 8.7kbps.

Synch Up

802.11 is a wireless standard, or protocol, that lets you connect computers to a network for sharing files and Internet connections. 802.11b transfers data at a maximum rate of 11mbps. 802.11a, a more recently introduced technology, transfers data at a maximum speed of 54mbps.

Wireless Security

Wireless local area networks (LANs) are easy to set up, and they are considerably easier for a smart hacker to break into than cable-based networks. If you are considering installing a wireless network, first decide how hack-worthy the information on your network is. Home users surfing the Net on two computers have less to fear than a company with sensitive documents on the network. Wireless protocols offer *encryption* (encoding data to make it harder to read), but they're still easier to break into than an Ethernet network.

Well-Connected Words

Encryption is a process that converts data into a scrambled code so that it cannot easily be intercepted without authorization.

Without adequate protection, accessing a wireless network could mean simply walking near your office or home with a laptop and wireless networking card.

Synch Up

Most notebooks now ship with infrared (IR) receivers. These can be a great help on the road, enabling you to use wireless mice, printers, and other peripherals without having to cart around wires. You can even synch up data to a desktop PC.

If you have sensitive data to protect, you need a knowledgeable system administrator to put in adequate protection. This is one place where knowing just a little about wireless technology can be dangerous.

Talk to a savvy network administrator if you're worried about your data. There's always some risk, but there's no need to worry unnecessarily. Your means of protection should be at a level that corresponds to your perceived risk.

Satellite vs. Cable or DSL

Wireless Internet access through satellite is especially promising for folks with no other options for broadband access. For rural customers with high-speed needs, two-way satellite is a real breakthrough.

However, for those with the option of getting DSL or cable access, satellite is much less attractive in price. Satellite providers, at press time, charge customers the price of equipment (which is somewhere in the neighborhood of $200), and still charge more per month than cable or DSL.

In addition, satellite providers typically require a professional to install the dish. Setting up a cable or DSL modem, on the other hand, should be quite simple, especially when you can just plug a cable or DSL modem into a USB connection on your PC or Macintosh.

When satellite access becomes more prevalent, the price will drop. But for now, cable and DSL are still the price leaders for broadband access.

Watch Out!

Although mobile wireless broadband is promising, it does have its limits. Two-way satellite isn't yet offered for those on the move, so they can't be used by people who'd like to take their broadband with them, as some folks with RVs do with satellite television. Because the antenna transmits as well as receives data, it's hard to install and is requested by the manufacturers to be done by a pro.

Going Wireless When Wired Will Do

As we've seen in this chapter, there are plenty of instances where wireless technology still needs to move past its growing pains. Customer demand hasn't yet met expectations, though it's sure to grow in the next few years.

With improved technology and greater coverage, competition will cut costs and improve performance. Wireless technology might be the wave of the future, but there are times when cutting the cord just doesn't make sense.

Incompatibility

There are increasing numbers of wireless standards, and most of them can't talk with each other. Wireless networking technologies that use radio signals to transmit data, such as *802.11b* and *HomeRF*, are incompatible with each other (and they can't communicate with the irDA infrared standard, found on laptops). These are just a handful of promising technologies—there are many others—that we've discussed that can't interoperate.

> **Well-Connected Words**
>
> **HomeRF** is a wireless local area network (LAN) protocol that transfers data at 1.6mbps. Like 802.11b and OpenAir, HomeRF equipment transmits in the 2.4GHz range. HomeRF is often cited for its ability to broadcast both voice and data. **OpenAir** is wireless networking technology, like HomeRF and 802.11b (Wi-Fi) transfers data at 1.6mbps and operates in the 2.4GHz band. **802.11b,** sometimes called Wi-Fi, is a wireless standard, or protocol, that enables you to connect computers to a network. You can find 802.11b devices at most electronics or computer stores. The standard makes it easy to set up a network that you can use to share files between computers or share an Internet connection. We'll talk more about this in Chapter 13.

Because of these incompatibilities, some technologies will fail to entice users and will drop out of the market. Others will coexist, as they meet different needs, but will still cause confusion in the buying public. Until the market matures, consumers will be unable to easily share date between mobile phones, PDAs, desktop computers, and laptops that use different wireless technologies.

Bet You Didn't Know

You probably have seen ads for Apple Computer's AirPort, which is an 802.11b device that, among other uses, enables you to walk around the house with a laptop and surf the Web. For PCs, equivalent devices are made by a number of manufacturers, including Lucent, Linksys, and Netgear. You insert an 802.11b card in a laptop's PC Card slot (or install a card into your desktop computer), plug in the wireless access point that sends data to and receives data from the computer, and you're set.

The Least You Need to Know

- ◆ Currently available wireless modems are often considerably slower than standard analog dial-up modems.

- ◆ Using wireless technology can mean tradeoffs. The mobility a wireless modem provides is offset if you can't connect or connections are slower than you need.

- ◆ Wireless broadband access is growing, but coverage in areas outside cities is still limited and likely will be for some time.

- ◆ Many wireless technologies, such as 802.11b, HomeRF, and IrDA, cannot communicate with each other.

Unplug and Stay Connected

In This Chapter

- ◆ Your mobile options
- ◆ Mobile add-ons
- ◆ Checking out wireless networking
- ◆ Staying put and going wireless

In this chapter we'll look at the best ways to get your work done, wirelessly, in different situations in which you might find yourself. Later in the book we'll check out each technology individually and provide more hands-on tips and how-to advice. Consider this dipping your foot into the pool of wireless computing.

Wireless technology is, of course, a natural for road trips. Whether you're roaming for profit or fun, there are a lot of decisions to make about which devices can best fit your needs and budget. We'll examine the best bets for staying in touch with the office, or just keeping up with the folks back home. In the process, we'll try and help you avoid getting lost, because wireless technology is pretty handy at both locating you and giving out directions.

Synch Up

Catching up on your favorite Web sites with a PDA is a great way to kill some time. Enter AvantGo (www.avantgo.com), a free service that enables you to view sites like *The Wall Street Journal* and the Weather Channel among many others. Is your PDA still modemless? You can download sites using AvantGo to a PDA and read them later.

Because, as we've talked about, wireless is good for travel and for the office (or home office), we'll consider connecting your computers to a local area network without drilling holes in the wall.

Taking the Net on the Road: Mobile Options

Ah, the joys of the open road. Flight delays. Rubberized chicken. Hotel phone rates. Thankfully, wireless computing can help you with all of these (well, you might be on your own with the chicken, unless you quietly e-mail a pizza place that delivers to a hotel ballroom).

In addition, if you travel for any length of time for business, you probably need to stay in touch back at the office by phone and e-mail and perhaps get some work done on a flight. Depending on your budget, you might find one device or a handful to take care of your work-related needs.

If You Need E-Mail Only

Your needs are simple. Hey, no problem. We can deal with that. You want e-mail on the go, and there are plenty of hardware and software providers that want to help you get connected (see Figure 3.1 for an example).

Two-way pagers are both hip and functional. You can fit one in your pocket, and they have the range of, well, pagers, a mature technology that won't leave you hanging.

Mobile phones can be a good option as well, because the prices keep dropping and because they offer good value for the money. Of course, smart phones as well as PDAs (see Figure 3.2) with wireless modems have more to offer than just e-mail, and we cover those in a bit.

Figure 3.1

A wireless BlackBerry hand-held lets you send and receive e-mail on the road.

(Photo courtesy of Research in Motion Limited)

Figure 3.2

A typical PDA.

If You Need E-Mail and Web Surfing

You're on the run a lot, and your business requires Web research. Some two-way pagers offer text-based Web access, but if you use the Web every day, you're likely to need something a little more sophisticated.

Laptops enable you to surf the Web and download important files. You have the desktop applications you need and you're portable (as long as you don't forget to charge your batteries the night before you take off).

If a laptop is too bulky for your needs, and you use Microsoft Windows and want to be able to work on Microsoft Word and Excel files, you might want to consider a Pocket PC, such as the Jornada from Hewlett Packard or the iPaq from Compaq.

> ### Synch Up
>
> Pocket PC is Microsoft's name for handheld computers that run the Pocket PC operating system (or the OS formerly known as Windows CE, version 3.0). The devices typically come with a stylus and compete with the Palm OS handhelds. Color screens are the norm for Pocket PCs these days, but you won't likely find a keyboard on the devices (although you might be able to connect one separately). Microsoft considers Windows CE devices with mini-keyboards, sometimes called clamshell devices, "handheld PCs."

Anyone who travels for business should have a mobile phone. To browse the Web, you need one that's WAP capable. WAP stands for the Wireless Application Protocol; it's a standard, like HTML, that allows Internet devices to view the Web on small screens.

Most of the advertising you love on the Web is missing (what a shame!) when you use a mobile phone to surf the Web. Instead of full Web pages, typically you'll see minimal graphics, which will let you access more quickly the information you want, such as your bank balance or a stock quote.

Using the keypad, you can punch in usernames and passwords, and Web-ready mobile phones usually have up and down buttons for scrolling and highlighting items as you browse. Most of the WAP-capable Web sites make your browsing easier by adding their most common features to a menu that you can click, instead of mangling your fingers trying to type.

That said, you can actually type with a phone. Click the 2 key twice, for instance, and you'll get a "b" (once for "a," three times for "c").

Most phones offer their own systems for making it easier to input characters. Incorporating the cursor helps, so that you can choose the letter or number you want from a menu. Symbols are also placed on menus, so you can peck in an @ symbol or a hyphen—any key from the keyboard.

Of course, it's a bit of a hassle to use a phone to send e-mails, so you probably won't be writing about how your vacation is going by phone. Instead, consider purchasing a serial cable for your cell phone that enables you to connect it to your laptop. You're sure to appreciate the little keys on your notebook after suffering through the keys on your phone.

If You Need E-Mail, Web, and Voice

Just about every digital mobile phone sold today offers some sort of Internet access. You won't have a hard time finding a phone that can also pick up your e-mail. The following is a list of common e-mail addresses for Internet-capable mobile phones.

Phone Type	E-Mail Address
AT&T	yourphonenumber@mobile.att.net
Cingular	yourphonenumber@mobile.mycingular.net
Metrocall	yourphonenumber@page.metrocall.com
Verizon	username@myvzw.com
Sprint PCS	yourphonenumber@messaging.sprintpcs.com
Nextel	yourphonenumber@messaging.nextel.com (two-way)
Voicestream	yourphonenumber@voicestream.net

And despite being less-feature filled than a laptop or PDA, a mobile phone can be a pretty handy way to stay in touch. You might not want to peck at your number keys to send a message. Yet picking up an important e-mail, followed by a return phone call is a reliable way to communicate on the road—and your boss and colleagues will respect your take charge attitude and quick responses.

If you need voice as well as Web and e-mail communications and you want a good organizer, you might consider a phone that includes a full-featured PDA, such as the Palm OS smart phones from Kyocera and Samsung, and the Nokia Communicator, which runs the highly regarded Symbian operating system.

Users give high marks to the phones for their portability and ease of use. These phones cost, as you might expect, more than a typical Internet-capable phone, and since fewer models are available, you'll have less choice when you shop for a wireless service provider.

You can also purchase expansion cards for the Handspring Visor PDA, which turns this organizer into a mobile phone, and provide Internet access and capability for short text messaging. The cards slide into the back of the Handspring and include an antenna for making calls. The whole thing is a bit bulky, but it makes for interesting conversations on the train to work.

Not to be outdone, Microsoft offers a mini version of its Internet Explorer browser, called Mobile Internet Explorer, on some mobile phones, including Mitsubishi's Trium Mondo (which is, unfortunately, not yet sold in the United States but might be in the future). Microsoft has an ambitious plan to bring mobile versions of its Windows operating system to consumers through phone makers and wireless service providers.

Synch Up

A recent study suggests that you might be carrying more than one handheld device in the future. The study (conducted by marketing research and consulting firm Yankelovich) says 53 percent of respondents would carry more than one handheld device if cost were of no concern. Most people (82 percent) wanted a wireless phone, while 35 percent desired a wireless e-mail device, and 30 percent wanted a PDA.

Adding Mobile Accessories

Business travelers who can't live without their PDAs are likely to invest in a mobile accessory or two. Along with add-ons that turn your PDA into a camera, a portable MP3-playing stereo, or an electronic-book reader, there are plenty of add-ons for getting your wireless work done. It's the age-old question: Should I turn my phone into a PDA, or turn my PDA into a phone? If your PDA accepts expansion cards (not all do) you can still add accessories through the phone's serial port. Here are just a few wireless *a la carte* items for your PDA:

- ◆ **Wireless modem.** You can pick up e-mail and view WAP and Web pages or send short text messages via the Internet.

◆ **Wireless network card.** When you return from your trip, a network card can help you jump onto your network without plugging in a cable to access data or synch up contacts or your calendar. Handspring offers a "module" for wireless network connections that slide into the Visor's expansion slot.

◆ **GPS.** Vendors including Delorme, GeoDiscovery (see Figure 3.3), and Garmin make handheld or dashboard global positioning system (GPS) devices you can connect to a laptop or PDA. These are handy for road trips, where you can plot a route and get on-the-fly information, such as your speed, position, and the next turn on your trip. The software shipped with your GPS system is also likely to include some extras like listings of restaurants and lodging, so you can find a good burrito at 12 A.M. in Tucson and avoid wrong turns on the way.

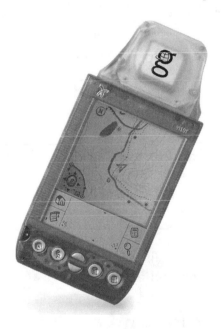

Figure 3.3

The GeoDiscovery Geode GPS device attaches to a Handspring Visor PDA.

Creating a Wireless Local Area Network

Creating a wireless network can be an incredibly handy way to get your work done more quickly. If you're still walking files around your office (a.k.a. SneakerNet), let me bend your ear about the benefits of working wirelessly.

The 802.11b standard (also called Wi-Fi) is currently the most popular way to create a wireless local area network. The technology allows you to use equipment from different manufacturers to connect computers together. It's not hard to set up 802.11b equipment, which has made devices using the standard very popular among home and office users.

Watch Out!

Although the maximum range of wireless networks is typically 300 feet (outdoors), most provide good results up to about 150 feet indoors, depending on the number of obstructions, including walls, concrete, steel, and possible interference from other household electronics that use the same radio frequency.

Traditional wired networks typically take quite a while to construct, because you need to install cards (sometimes called *network adapters* or *network interface cards*) in each computer and connect all of them with cables.

With a wireless network, you see two obvious advantages:

◆ No unsightly wires

◆ The ability to move computers at will, even take them outside, and still stay connected

As in life, there's usually some bad news with the good. Wireless networks are expensive. Expect to spend quite a bit more per computer you want to connect wirelessly.

Also, you need to use passwords on your network (the good kind, not ones found in the dictionary) because anybody with an 802.11b card walking by your office on a laptop can hop right onto your network if it's not password protected. There are other security issues, which we'll address in Chapter 14, "Maintaining Wireless Networks."

Okay, with that warning issued, let's keep in mind that wireless networks are really handy and secure if you take precautions.

Different Kinds of Wireless Networks

If you've decided to network your computers wirelessly, you might first want to consider the available technologies. What's that, you say? There's more than one? There are, at this writing, five commonly used technologies for networking wirelessly, and you might see any or all at your local computer store.

All the technologies work similarly. Each broadcasts a radio signal that can travel a set distance, through walls and other obstructions. The main differences are in speed, because each of the protocols have a maximum (best-case scenario) range of about 300 feet, over which they broadcast a signal to your computers.

As you start shopping around for wireless network equipment, you'll come across some new jargon. None of it is wildly complicated, you just need to know the lingo. Let's translate:

- **IEEE 802.11.** This protocol is one of several wireless LAN standards from the Institute of Electrical and Electronics Engineers (IEEE). 802.11 transfers data at 2 megabits per second (mbps), but you're less likely to run into it, than 802.11b, which is more widely used (and faster).

- **IEEE 802.11b.** This is the wireless technology that has the widest current acceptances. Despite being competitively priced, 802.11b moves data much faster than other common wireless networking protocols, at a maximum of 11mbps.

- **IEEE 802.11a.** This protocol operates at a very fast 24mbps (and potentially up to 54mbps) but is not yet widely available. 802.11a operates in the cleaner, less-crowded 5GHz band.

- **OpenAir.** This protocol transfers data at 1.6mbps and operates in the 2.4GHz band.

- **HomeRF.** This protocol transfers data at 1.6mbps. Like 802.11a and OpenAir, this wireless networking technology transmits in the 2.4GHz range. HomeRF is often cited for its ability to broadcast both voice and data.

> **CAUTION**
>
> **Watch Out!**
>
> Wireless Networks operate in the 2.4GHz range and can be disrupted by other electronics that use the same range. Cordless phones and microwaves, for example, can cause interruptions over a wireless network.

Soup to Nuts: Wireless Network Hardware

To get started, you need network cards for each computer you want to connect. You can also purchase an *access point*, which connects the wireless network to an existing wired network. When speaking of wireless networks,

Well-Connected Words

An **access point** is a wireless networking device lets you tie a wireless network into a wired network. An access point communicates with the wireless networking cards you install in each computer in a network.

I concentrate on 802.11b technology because it's speedy enough for most Web surfing needs, reasonably priced, and the most prevalent of the wireless networking technologies.

The wireless access point can also include a router, which enables you to connect a number of different computers to the same Internet connection. In the case of the Apple AirPort, for instance (an 802.11b device), several computers can share the included 56kbps modem. You can also use the AirPort to share a cable or DSL Internet connection among all the computers in a home or office.

After you have a wireless access point, you can start adding computers to the network. To do this, you install an 802.11b device to each computer that you want to add to the network.

The device could plug into the USB port on a computer, or it might be a PC Card that slides into the PC Card port on a computer. You can also buy a PCI card that you insert into a desktop computer, and then slide the 802.11b PC Card into that.

In the making-your-life-easier department, many new laptops offer wireless home networking gear as an option when you buy.

Bet You Didn't Know

By 2003, 1.5 million homes will use wireless networking technology, according to research firm The Yankee Group.

In the end, making the decision to go wireless has much to do with determining what equipment is right for you. If your office is fairly small, an Ethernet network is the inexpensive, if less futuristic, choice. If wiring an office will take too long or is too unsightly, a wireless network might make more sense.

Check, Please: Wireless Network Expenses

Now, for the bill. As we mentioned, wireless networks can be a little pricey. By the time you read this book, costs will undoubtedly have dropped. But wireless networks, per machine, always cost more than wired networks, because more sophisticated equipment is required.

As of this writing, setting up an 802.11b wireless network runs you about $100 per PC, whereas Ethernet cards typically cost around $20. Not so bad in a home office but hard to justify in a small-to-medium businesses with tight budgets.

Setting Up a Wireless Network

Now it's time to take a look at the overall steps you take when setting up a wireless network. Keep in mind that a wired network provides less flexibility than a wireless network. But with a wireless network, you need to carefully consider where you're placing your computers. You lose speed as components are placed farther from each other.

> **Synch Up**
> Both HomeRF and Wi-Fi are working on speedier versions of their networking protocols. HomeRF will soon transmit data at 10mbps (up from 1.6mpbs) in its second version. Wi-Fi is looking to jump ahead of its competitor, by going to 54mbps in a future version. But for now, 802.11b is the most popular, and fastest, wireless networking standard.

Here are the basic steps for installing a wireless network, connected to a broadband Internet connection:

1. Plug a network access point into an Ethernet hub or router (which allows several computers to access the Internet).
2. Plug a cable or DSL modem into the hub or router.
3. Install a wireless network card into each computer that needs to be connected.
4. Install the software that comes with your hardware.
5. Test your network.

The Linksys wireless access point (see Figure 3.4) includes a router and print server. The router allows multiple computers to access the same Internet connection. The print server lets the wirelessly networked computers share a printer.

So now you know the basic steps for setting up a wireless network. Of course, you need to give some thought to which vendor to purchase from, and you need to do some shopping around for the best price.

Figure 3.4

The Linksys wireless access point.

In Chapter 13, "Starting a Wireless Network," we spend more time delving into the wonderful world of wireless networks, trying to head off some potential installation hang-ups, and giving you some hands-on advice so that you can get going on your own. And that's what wireless technology is all about, right? Increased freedom, whether it's freedom from cables or the smug looks of your more computer literate friends.

Bet You Didn't Know

You can find 802.11b networks at hotels and airports, where you can rent access to broadband Internet access. Also getting into the action is coffee chain Starbucks, which plans to offer wireless access in some of its franchises. College campuses are taking advantage of wireless network technology, and some are offering access wherever students roam on school grounds. In spring of 2001, Dartmouth installed a campus-wide 802.11b network with access points placed strategically so students and faculty can access the network or use the Internet wirelessly.

The Least You Need to Know

◆ For e-mail on the road, consider a two-way pager. For text-based Web surfing, consider a PDA or mobile phone. For e-mail and full-featured Web surfing, a laptop or PDA is your best bet.

◆ Of the five available wireless technologies, 802.11b currently offers the most bang for the buck. Future versions of the protocol Home RF will give 802.11b, sometimes called Wi-Fi, a run for its money.

◆ To set up a wireless network that connects to the Internet, you need a network access point; a PCI, USB, or PC Card wireless adapter for each computer you want to connect; and an (inexpensive) Ethernet hub.

◆ Wireless networks cost more than inexpensive Ethernet (wired) networks.

◆ A wired network provides less flexibility than a wireless network. But with a wireless network, you need to carefully consider where you're placing your computers—you lose speed as components are placed farther from each other.

Chapter 4

Research and Buying

In This Chapter

- ◆ How to spend smartly on wireless
- ◆ Considering your current hardware
- ◆ Checking out wireless networking
- ◆ Finding bargains

With such a wide range of wireless mobile and stationary technologies available, choosing a wireless device can be intimidating. Often your choice is determined by how much you can spend.

In this chapter we'll consider what will fit your budget and offer up recommendations. If you're the sort of adventurous early adopter who says things like "I remember using nanotechnology back when it was cool," you will get less use from this chapter than a thrifty owner of a five-year-old PC. If you find yourself saying "I'd like a handheld organizer, but there are too many models available, and I don't want to spend a lot," we welcome you to the club of cautious buyers.

Throughout this chapter, we'll consider your existing hardware, because it might serve you as well as, or better than, what you'd spend to upgrade your equipment to the latest and greatest. And while we like to save a buck, it's important to find tools that will last. Spending a little more for the available device can help you stay in business longer and with less frustration. All that—and more handy wireless tips and advice—is coming right up in this next exciting episode.

Budget This: How Much Can You Spend?

Let's take a look at what you've got lying around your desk. After this quick inventory, we can suggest a device or add-on to make connecting wirelessly, at home or on the road, a straightforward proposition.

A small amount of pre-planning can help you avoid some costly mistakes in the future. Technology changes quickly, especially wireless technology, but you can insure yourself against buying obsolete equipment before you open the box by becoming informed on what's available.

If You Have a Cell Phone

You own the cornerstone of modern wireless technology. It's a good start, and depending on the kind you have, you have lots of options, including:

- **WAP surfing.** There's a distinction between Web surfing and WAP surfing that should be explained. To surf the Web, you need a browser that can read HTML (Hypertext Markup Language) pages. On your desktop computer and your laptop, you might use Internet Explorer or Netscape to view HTML pages. Most phones, however, use a WAP (Wireless Application Protocol) browser. WAP browsers view pages written in WML (Wireless Markup Language) specially created pages for small screens that use minimal graphics, to make the best use of the slower speeds of wireless cellular networks you can access on the road.

- **Send e-mail.** You can send and receive e-mail on your phone, though you can't send attachments.

◆ **Connect to a laptop.** Purchase a cable for your phone, and you can probably connect it to your laptop. The cell phone acts as a wireless modem. Connecting your phone to your computer in this way can save you the cost of purchasing a separate wireless modem, which plugs into the *PC Card expansion slot* of your laptop.

Well-Connected Words

A PC Card expansion slot, sometimes called PCMCIA, enables you to add peripherals to your laptop, such as wireless modems, networking cards, and nonwireless gear like removable storage and memory.

If you haven't yet purchased your phone, seriously consider shopping for one that enables you to connect it to your laptop or PDA. This option vastly increases the number of ways you can use your phone wirelessly. Ask a salesperson at your local wireless dealer or an online shop to price several phones with connection cables for you.

A cell phone with the ability to read e-mail and surf the Web could do the job. If you combine a Web phone with a good long distance calling plan, you might have all the hardware and service you require.

With a capable wireless phone you can browse the Internet and send and receive e-mail. If you connect your Web phone by cable to a laptop, you can even dial up your office network remotely (computers running Windows 95 and later have this capability built-in). Sounds great, right? The catch is that most people aren't satisfied with the no-nonsense Web browsing and small, colorless screen seen on many Web phones. If those features do not impress you, your mood won't change when you try entering a 14-character Web address with a numeric keypad. In the next section, we look at some of the ways to throw a laptop into the picture and get some work done with the wireless Internet.

Synch Up

YouCanWorkFrom Anywhere.com (YCWFA) provides articles and tips for folks who work from home and on the road. You can subscribe (and unsubscribe) to the site's free newsletter at www.ycwfa.com/newsletters. www.YouCanWorkFromAnywhere. com/rwarchives also offers an archive.

If You Have a Laptop

Now you're cooking with gas. You have the basic computing power to really get some work done remotely or roam around your home or office and potentially eliminate the need to jack into phone lines, network connections, and outlets while you work.

Watch Out!

Most laptops sold in the last few years come with an internal or PC Card modem, so it's possible to connect your existing modem to an analog cellular phone, with the right cable. I pride myself on being a sort of wireless Bob Villa, connecting my cell phone to my lawn mower or turning the rice cooker into a wireless Internet terminal. Hooking up your laptop's modem to a cell phone is tricky, in other words. Importantly, you can't use your laptop's internal, analog modem (the one it likely came with) to connect to the Internet over a *digital* cellular phone, which is the most common type of phone sold today, since digital phones often offer Internet access and more clarity than older analog models.

If you haven't yet shopped for a cell phone, look for one that also acts as a modem. You're limited to speeds around 14.4kbps, but that's fine for quick e-mails and limited surfing.

Your existing laptop might have a built-in infrared port for sending and receiving data wirelessly. These ports can be a handy way to synch up the data on a PDA to a desktop (without using the PDA's cradle) or send a document to a printer with an infrared port. You can purchase inexpensive adapters for infrared transmission if you want to use infrared technology with your desktop computer.

For high-speed, wireless access to your home or office network, an 802.11b PC Card is your best bet—for now. In the next year we'll see major improvements in speed for all the wireless network technology; but 802.11b, also known as Wi-Fi, is the most widely adopted. Wireless network cards are increasingly sold bundled with new laptops, and Apple has offered them for several years with its AirPort products.

> **CAUTION**
>
> **Watch Out!** _____
>
> Worried about the radiation levels from your mobile phone? You're not alone. The major phone manufacturers have agreed to add labels that rate cell phone frequency emissions. The Cellular Telecommunications Industry Association will no longer certify phones that don't meet the new label requirement. Labels inside and outside of the phone's box tell consumers that the phone meets FDA and FCC radio frequency guidelines. CNET also offers charts of the 10 highest and lowest radiation cell phones at wireless.cnet.com.

If You Have a PDA

You've already taken the plunge, and now you can't find anything without your PDA. Of course, you don't have to limit the use of your assistant to just storing contact information, crunching numbers, and taking notes.

Add a wireless modem, and you can hop onto the Web and fire off e-mail, check out movie listings, directions, sports scores, and all sorts of Web information on the run.

Add a wireless networking card, and you have access to your network at high speed; you can kiss your cradle good-bye.

If You Have an Existing Network

Your office is already wired. That's okay. Wireless networking is designed to slip into the wired world and does so quite easily.

The wireless access point (sometimes called an AP) helps bridge a wireless network with a wired one. We'll cover this in some detail in Chapter 13, "Starting a Wireless Network." The access point typically includes an Ethernet port for connecting to a traditional wired Ethernet network. You can plug the Ethernet port into a variety of wired Ethernet network hardware, including:

◆ An Ethernet hub, for connecting several computers in an existing wired network

◆ A cable or DSL modem, for fast access to the Internet

◆ A router, for sharing one Internet connection among two or more computers

Add a network card to your PDA, laptop, or desktop and you can jump right onto your existing network and start roaming around the office, between floors, without losing your connection (well, up to a point). If you get more than 150 feet—perhaps less depending on obstructions—away from the access point, you'll be hard pressed to keep up a good connection.

I Don't Have That: Deciding What You Need

Now that you know what you've got, it's a good time to consider what you need. This section offers a handful of suggestions to help you shop smartly while you're looking for hardware and services.

Whether you need a phone, PDA, two-way pager, laptop, or network, you can buy confidently, knowing that you've done your legwork. And it's always good to make the salespeople sweat a little.

What to Look for in Phones

When shopping for a new phone, consider screen size, Web capability, and cost. Screens on Internet-capable phones, sometimes called smart phones, are, in a word, tiny, but manufacturers are getting the picture and increasing the number of lines you can view when browsing Web sites.

Synch Up

If getting away from the office is a permanent choice, check out The Hartman Research Group at www. hartmanresearch.com. The organization keeps a list of companies that are telecommuter friendly. They can even help you develop your resumé for firms with telecommuting programs.

Most Internet-capable mobile phones, or smart phones, include PDA-like abilities, including synching mail and calendar entries from a desktop or laptop Personal Information Manager (PIM), such as Microsoft Outlook. Often used to mean digital cellular, *personal communications services* (*PCS*) offer a range of services, including voicemail, caller ID, and Internet access. Be mindful that potential data rates are quite a bit different than what an Internet service provider might support. A wireless phone might offer speeds comparable to a 56kbps modem, but most wireless service providers max out at 14.4kbps.

Keeping in mind the difference between the phone's capabilities and the offerings of a service provider, hop on the Web and check out several service providers' Web sites to see what data rates you can get from the phone you want.

What to Look for in PDAs

If you're a business traveler, it's hard to resist the call of the personal data assistant. Mild mannered at first blush, with the right components, they become wired gateways to all the information you forgot back at the office.

The Palm VII may appeal to some as the older member of the wirelessly connected PDA crowd. The organizer was one of the first on the scene to surf the Internet, using a built-in modem that operates at 8.7kbps, and skips banner advertisements and unnecessary graphics.

Well-Connected Words

PCS (**personal communications services**) refers to both voice and data services, such as voicemail, caller ID, and wireless Internet access, communicating in the 1,900MHz band. Often used to mean digital cellular, PCS offers a range of services, including voicemail, caller ID, and Internet access.

While a built-in modem has its appeal, an expansion slot is more helpful, since you can keep up with the latest technologies by dropping in a new modem or GPS. All the major PDA makers now offer models with ports for peripherals.

An entry level Palm or PocketPC will likely skimp on color and memory. More expensive models will throw in color screens and more storage. Again, here's where an expansion card makes sense. You can add in a wireless network card, or pop in a memory card to increase the data you can store.

What to Look for in a Two-Way Pager

Two-way pagers effectively address a common complaint about Web-browsing on mobile phones and (some) PDAs: There's no keyboard. True, the keyboard might be small, but for sending a quick message ("Home in 1 minute"), they're awfully handy.

Synch Up

Here are just a handful of airports with wireless network access. The list grows nearly daily, so for more—and more current—listings, check www.mobilestar.net and www.wayport.net. In addition to those listed here, many more airports offer wireless access in private airline lounges.

- Austin-Bergstrom International Airport
- Dallas-Fort Worth International Airport
- Seattle-Tacoma International Airport
- San Jose International Airport
- SDF Louisville Airport
- Sioux Falls Regional Airport
- PIT AA Pittsburgh

The two-way pagers discussed in this book all include some sort of *QWERTY* keyboard and a pointing device. Most enable you to browse text-based Web pages and send quick text messages to a server that responds with a stock quote, the current weather or other requested information.

Well-Connected Words

The **QWERTY** keyboard takes its name from the top-left six keys of most keyboards. Invented in 1868 by Christopher Sholes, who also invented the typewriter, the QWERTY keyboard is still the most popular in use. Some say the configuration of letters was created to slow down fast typists and keep the keys from jamming. Others say this story behind the design of the keyboard is just a myth.

Most often you see the small two-way pagers such as those from Research in Motion (the BlackBerry handheld) and the Motorola models (such as the Talkabout). A clamshell design is common, with the small screen flipping down for travel. However, manufacturers are adding two-way paging into all sorts of devices, including tablet-shaped computers that also act as PDAs. Some watches are even getting in on the action (though they can only receive, not send, messages).

Cost and design vary so widely; you need make the very personal decision of what shape and price work best for you.

The most important pager decision you make is selecting a service plan. Most providers promote some sort of unlimited service, but all-you-can page messaging isn't cheap. If you can't see paying the unlimited fee, you have to choose a more limited plan that restricts the number of characters you send and receive. But watch out for a whopping bill at the end of the month if you exceed the character limit.

What to Look for in Laptops

Just about any laptop made in the last few years can handle most wireless computing tasks. For browsing the Web, picking up e-mail, pulling data off your network, and sending documents to a shared printer, you might choose to shop for used equipment in good condition. You can certainly accomplish any of these tasks with a laptop that costs less than $1,000, sometimes much less, if you're willing to use a smaller screen, slower processor, and smaller hard drive.

More recent laptops are likely to include an infrared port for trading data with a desktop PC, sending jobs to infrared-enabled printers (such as models made by Hewlett Packard). You can synch your calendar on your laptop or send a contact's phone number to a mobile phone.

For wireless networking, some laptops feature a built-in 802.11b device, such as the iBooks from Apple. You can use these when traveling, too, connecting to a wireless network at some hotels, coffee shops, and airports.

The Psion (see Figure 4.1) is an example of an *EPOC*-based PDA with support for *Bluetooth* wireless technology. The EPOC operating system from Symbian is used in handhelds and mobile phones. The OS can be used to connect to the Internet and synch data with computers. EPOC supports the Wireless Application Protocol (WAP), Bluetooth, and Java.

Well-Connected Words

EPOC is an operating system from Symbian used in handhelds and mobile phones to access the Internet and synch devices with computers. EPOC supports the Wireless Application Protocol (WAP), Bluetooth, and Java. **Bluetooth** is a fast (720Kbps) method of transferring data short distances from mobile devices, such as laptops and PDAs, to desktop computers.

Figure 4.1

The Psion handheld is an EPOC-based PDA with support for Bluetooth wireless technology.

What to Look for in a Wireless Network

We've tended to focus on one type of wireless network, 802.11b, because it's both fast and reasonably priced. Before you connect, though, there are a few options to consider.

All the currently available wireless local area networking (LAN) technologies, including OpenAir and Home RF, transfer data at least 1.6mbps. That speed exceeds most of the current broadband Internet connections found in most homes and offices. What's that mean? For browsing the Web, any of the available wireless options will do.

For transferring data across a network, you'll want as much speed as you can get, however. That's why 802.11b has an edge: It runs at 11 mbps, which means faster file transfers and printing.

Other promising technologies include Bluetooth, a Personal Area Networking (PAN) technology, which like 802.11b, operates in the 2.4GHz band and is a good choice for temporarily connecting PDAs, like the Compaq iPaq, to desktop computers and laptops. And, if you can wait, manufacturers should soon start to deliver wireless networking products based on the 802.11a standard, which offers maximum data rates of 54mbps.

Keep in mind that traditional wired networks are still faster: Most Ethernet networks have a maximum throughput of 100mbps. If wireless networking appeals to you, consider using a mixed environment. That is, keep computers connected by Ethernet for most of your heavy-duty jobs, such as running applications off a server or transferring files. Mix in wireless networking for laptops that need mobility, or connect a computer in an office where it's a pain to run cable.

Synch Up

Shopping around for a mobile phone and PDA? If your needs are simple, you might do just fine with an Internet-capable smart phone. Increasingly, mobile phones are available with sophisticated, PDA-like abilities, including voice dialing, e-mail, Web browsing, and features for synchronizing data, such as addresses and calendars with desktop computers.

Where to Buy

Now that your head is swimming with wireless products to buy, and you've got enough information to ask some good questions (or send some smart e-mails), let's figure out where you should start.

Whether you prefer to shop online or, uh, off, I'll try to pass along some handy buying tips and advice. Trust me on this one: If you're at a Turkish market and the deal on the PDA looks too good to be true … it probably is. I learned that tidbit the hard way.

All right, let's get to shopping.

Considering Online Auctions

Wow, a new PDA for $6. It sounds great, of course, until you see that it's the current bidding price and the auction doesn't end for six days. The final price will be considerably higher, perhaps much higher, based on the enthusiasm, and feeding frenzy, that sometimes accompanies online bidding (see Figure 4.2).

Recently, I read an ad for a $10 PDA in such bad shape the seller said, without joking, that it would be "good for parts," as if you might fashion your own screen to replace the broken one, out of some old Palm Pilots in the shed.

Figure 4.2

Don't take the first offer: haggling over a Visor at Computers.com.

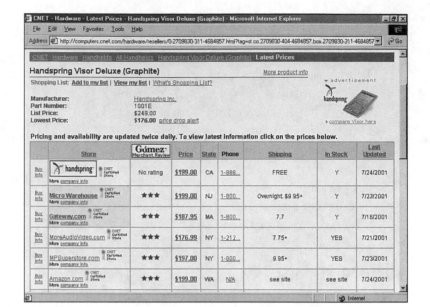

Figure 4.2

Don't take the first offer: haggling over a Visor at Computers.com.

Auction come-ons are more common than good deals. You'll need both luck and patience to do well at an auction, where overpaying is more typical—and frankly, part of the game—than a real bargain.

With the price of a PDA or laptop falling the minute after you buy, you might do better to check manufacturers' refurbished models, or buy a slightly older unit, to save a little bit of cash. However screens wear out over time, and a new, budget PDA is often a safer bet.

When searching for a new PDA, consider online price watchers. You can use a site, such as PriceWatch (www.pricewatch) and MySimon (www.mysimon. com), to get the best deal currently available. CNET (www.cnet.com) offers reviews and a price watching service; you can at least see the going rate for the model you want before you buy online or elsewhere.

Searching Online and Local Classifieds

Although you can sometimes find a good deal at auction sites, you might also benefit from instant purchase options. Popular online auction site eBay offers a service called half.com that allows sellers to list items, including many electronics, free.

Bet You Didn't Know

A small movement across the United States wants to give you access to the Internet, at broadband speeds, for free. Wireless communities are sprouting up in cities and small towns with big-hearted geeks who are trying to wire the world by thinking locally. There is a slightly ignoble aspect, however, because some in the free access community hop onto wide-open wireless networks and grab access on the sly. That's another good reason to secure the access point on your wireless network. Read the instructions that come with your access point so that you can turn on encryption, restrict access to a list of users you know, and take any other recommended steps to block it from unauthorized access. See Chapter 14, "Maintaining Wireless Networks," for more on wireless network security.

And just because this is the twenty-first century and we're all flying around with our jetpacks, don't forget to consider the local newspaper classifieds. I've picked up some pretty good deals from people who were moving up the electronics ladder.

Shopping at Electronics Stores

Visiting your local chain electronics store is a great way to get the lay of the land. You can put your hands on the little keyboards, check out the screens in dark and bright light, and generally find out problems you wouldn't notice until too late when you buy online.

Without a doubt, before you start shopping online, hit the bricks and mortar stores first, if you can. If you can't, online sellers usually offer a return policy, but nothing beats a little firsthand experience.

When shopping for wireless networking equipment in a local store, you can more quickly see what products are compatible, and ask a few questions about customer returns and satisfaction with whatever products you're considering.

You might even shock a salesperson by asking about the extended warranty. A $120 PDA is pretty likely to hit the ground at some point during your travels. See if a reasonably priced extended warranty covers accidental damage.

The Least You Need to Know

- When you start shopping for wireless equipment, consider building on what you have rather than replacing all your existing equipment.
- If you don't shop around and choose a service plan carefully—whether it's for a two-way pager, smart phone, or wireless modem—get ready for a mind-numbing monthly bill.
- You can integrate wireless LAN (local area network) technology into a wired network, giving you increased mobility and leaving the Ethernet to what it does best, transferring data very quickly.
- When it comes to finding bargains, the classified section is still a good bet, even in this online age.

Chapter 5

Serious Research: Finding More About Wireless Options

In This Chapter

- ◆ Wireless research
- ◆ Considering cost
- ◆ Tips from vendors and trade publications
- ◆ Finding help online

Online research is the cornerstone of a good wireless plan. The Internet allows you to load up advice from experts and regular folks before you settle on one technology, and then find the best deal for what you're planning to spend.

A little time online goes a long way. Information wants to be free, or so it's been said, and you can find plenty of good wireless buying advice, free of charge, on the Web. Of course, really good information wants a paycheck, so if you're considering a serious investment in wireless technology for your business or department, you might consider purchasing the report of a wireless analyst, which might help you get a better sense of the future of a technology before plunking down a purchase order.

The past few chapters covered the basic wireless technologies for mobile and stationary computing. Now let's look at getting good deals on those technologies, avoiding getting stuck with soon-to-be-obsolete equipment, and finding help after you've dug in.

Determining Expenses

To figure out what you're likely to spend, you might first check out the roundups of trade publications. An editor's choice on products from the major trade magazines is a likely bet for wireless equipment with good features at a fair price.

Prices listed for wireless equipment in trade magazines are typically higher than what you can find at online stores, due to the lead time magazines need to get to press (or publish on the Web). Retail prices are always quite a bit higher than street prices, so you should never end up paying the manufacturer's suggested retail price (MSRP).

When purchasing mobile devices, determining the cost often has more to do with monthly service prices rather than the start-up cost of the device. The old razor vs. razor blades analogy is useful here: You spend most of your money on refills; or, in the case of mobile wireless devices, you spend most of your money on service plans.

Bet You Didn't Know

Birds in Denmark and the United Kingdom are beginning to incorporate mobile phone ringers into the repertoire of songs. According to media reports, Danish ornithologists say the most likely bird to lift a wireless phone's song is the starling, which (no kidding) tends to favor the pleasing tones of a Nokia model.

Keep in mind while you're shopping for mobile wireless in particular, that the service provider you choose will be your most important decision. If your provider's coverage area is limited, it won't matter how cool your phone is. Likewise, if you can't find a monthly service plan that provides enough included minutes to get your work done, your phone will become an expensive paperweight.

Avoiding Mistakes

One of the most confusing aspects of wireless technology today is the ever-increasing number of standards. There are wireless networking standards, wireless modem standards, and two-way paging technologies. Which one to choose?

Well-Connected Words

IrDA refers to a handful of protocols that transmit data wirelessly from three to six feet. Data is transmitted at either 115.2kbps or 4mbps.

Avoiding incompatibility is key; you want to stay away from buying several devices to handle one task. Bluetooth and *IrDA* are incompatible ways of moving data between PCs, PDAs, and printers, among other devices. Consider choosing one or the other. (Currently, IrDA devices far outnumber ones using Bluetooth.) In other cases, buying multiple devices—a PDA and a mobile phone, for instance—might save you more money than purchasing an all-in-one device, like the pricey mobile phone/PDAs that have become common.

Finding the Best Bang for Your Buck

By scanning trade vendor sites, trade publications, and independent online sources, you can get a get a good idea of price and performance before you start shopping.

Each of these resources has its benefits. A trade magazine often provides the latest news, hands-on reviews, tutorials, and comparisons of different wireless products in a category. A newsgroup can help you get answers quickly from helpful readers. Analysts can provide you with a picture of a given market and help determine the future success or failure of technology you might be considering.

Trade Publications

Computer magazines tend to cover wireless technology with an eye toward working with applications as well as editing and transmitting documents rather than simply making voice calls.

Whether you're looking for a roundup of a whole range of technology, reviews of the latest gear, or news on upcoming technology, these sites can help you impress the members of your workgroup (or show your kids they're not the only ones who know how to use a computer).

When shopping around for equipment for your business, keep an eye out for magazines that cover your industry, which might offer more specific (and useful) wireless guidance for the type of work that you do. The general computing trade magazines make for a great read, but *Hot Beverage Monthly* (just an example) might be more keyed into your technology needs.

The following are helpful trade publications:

- ZDNet, now owned by CNET, offers a range of publications that deal with wireless computing. Reviews of hardware and recent pricing are available in a few clicks. Dig a little deeper, and you'll find ZDNet's Wireless Resource Center, which pulls together reviews and tips on one page. The wireless section has an unwieldy Web address, but you can easily search for it from the home page (www.zdnet.com).

- CNET produces many reviews of technology and hardware as well as how-to information and links to newsgroups that discuss technology and hardware. CNET's wireless page is found, not surprisingly, at wireless. cnet.com.

- IDG.net (see Figure 5.1) is the front door for dozens of computer publications (www.idg.net). From the main page (refer to the graphic that follows), you can search for information on networks, mobile phones, PDAs, and two-way pagers and find reports from standbys, including *Macworld* (published jointly by IDG and Ziff-Davis), *PC World*, and *Computerworld*.

- *Network Computing* at networkcomputing.com can get you up to speed, with articles and tutorials on the latest technology and devices for network information.

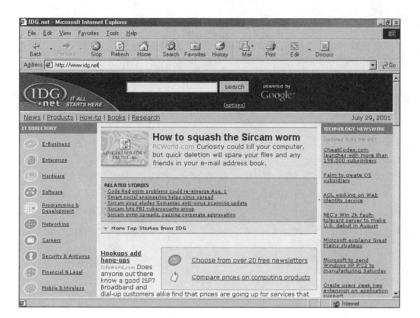

Figure 5.1

IDG's home page offers site-wide searching of its maga-zines, including PC World *and* Macworld.

Vendor Sites

When comparing products, go straight to the horse's mouth. The Web sites of wireless device manufacturers often give you the most up-to-date information on device capabilities, pricing, and technical specs.

Synch Up

The buying advice in these first few chapters, especially when discussing business equipment, presumes you have the authority to purchase and install new hardware at your location. If you're working in a company with an information technology department, make sure to see if a wireless initiative is already in progress. IT departments frown on folks installing their own hardware on the job. And since wireless networking equipment, in particular, is relatively inexpensive and simple to set up, this can be a very real headache for IT managers.

Just keep in mind that vendors tend to accentuate the positive. Mobile wireless providers typically highlight *maximum* data rates and coverage areas, which are best-case scenarios. Likewise, wireless home and office networking vendors tend to feature their products' maximum range, overlooking potential performance-degrading problems, such as interference or obstructions.

Surveying Independent Sources

Interested in more shoot-from-the-hip information? There's no shortage of well-informed wireless computing gurus logging their thoughts on the Web. These serve as a welcome dose to vendor sites' enthusiasm, and they're often the quickest way to find information.

Sources on the Internet come and go, but here is a quick sampling of places to add to your information diet:

- **Newsgroups.** alt.internet.wireless is a great place to start reading about wireless technology. If you don't have a configured newsreader, you can find postings on the Web at groups.google.com. Another benefit of using Google is its search feature, which can help you find the subject you're seeking in a flash. Comp.std.wireless is highly technical, though very informative. It's not a good place to throw out questions, but it's helpful for research, especially on the compatibility between technologies. At comp.std.wireless you can find lots of useful information on wireless networking and standards. For general network questions, including wireless networks, check out comp.dcom.lans.ethernet.

- **Newsletters.** CMP, another large computer trade publisher, sends out a biweekly mailing on wireless technologies, with short summaries and stories from its publications. Subscribe at www.techweb.com (another great place to search for news and reviews). CNET offers a handful of free tech newsletters at CNET help.com, including wireless and modem tips.

- **Web sites.** About.com offers helpful information on all types of subjects. Its computer-networking site (compnetworking.about.com/cs/ wirelesswap/) offers up-to-date information on wireless technologies from around the Web as well as information on wired networking. A broader range of wireless topics is discussed at wireless.about.com. You can find "News for Nerds" at Slashdot (slashdot.org) a well-respected site for its technology news and discussion. Check out the Technology section, where you'll find much information on wireless networking. Slashdot also has a handy search engine.

> **Watch Out!**
>
> Some of the e-mail lists in this book can get a bit overwhelming. You can sign up for a free account at www.mailshell. com that enables you to set up as many e-mail boxes as you want. You can set up mailboxes for each list you sign up to, using a different address for each one. Doing so can let you know if a certain company has sold your name to a marketing list and keeps your personal e-mail box from filling with junk e-mail.

Analysts

As you're about to pack up for a well-deserved weekend, your boss tells you that you need to create a purchasing and rollout plan for your wireless needs by Monday. After your pleasant daydream of strangling the boss runs its course, hop on the Web and find yourself an analyst's report. Some research is even available for free:

◆ ZDNet's (researchcenter.zdnet.com) research tool has free and fee-based research (see Figure 5.2). You can search for magazine articles, reports by analysts, and white papers.

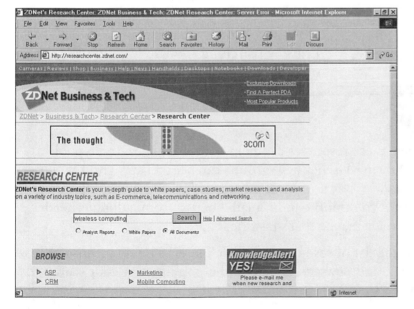

Figure 5.2

Get caught up with the latest at ZDNet's Research Center.

- Nua.com (www.nua.com) is a free online provider of market research. The Ireland-based company offers insight on technology from around the world. Here you can find just the right stat to impress the boss: "It says here we're 50 percent more likely to crush the competition if we employ fast wireless technology."

Other research comes at a (much) greater cost. Here are a just a few well-known research firms that can help you in a pinch:

- Forrester (www.forrester.com) is a well-known market research firm that helps companies integrate the Internet and other technologies into their businesses.
- Gartner (www.gartner.com) advises businesses and creates reports on information technology and forecasting technology market trends.
- The Yankee Group (www.yankeegroup.com) advises companies and provides research on electronic commerce, wireless technology, the Internet, and other technologies.
- Jupiter Media Metrix (www.jmm.com) provides analysis and advice on the Internet and new technology.

Watch Out!

If you plan to add wireless computing devices in your home or office, you might consider doing a little research on keeping your data safe.

Don't forget that you can find more research firms by searching Google (www.google.com) or Yahoo! (www.yahoo.com).

What to Do Now

When you get stuck, these resources can help you. Web sites, trade publications, and the all-knowing Usenet newsgroups can set you straight. Of course, if you're really stuck, why not use wireless technology to get yourself out of the office? Sometimes you think—and e-mail—better from a double-header down at the ballpark. Or maybe that's just me.

Keep in mind, that the list of resources in this chapter is by no means exhaustive. These sites, lists, and newsgroups should help jump-start your search to find your own trusted sources of information.

The Least You Need to Know

- ◆ Given the quick pace of technology and the wide range of technologies relating to wireless computing, a good bit of online research can help you before you buy equipment.

- ◆ A handful of trade publications dedicate good portions of their coverage to wireless technology these days. You can find new, hands-on reviews and newsletters that keep you in the know.

- ◆ Analyst reports might be pricey, but for company-wide decision making, they can be of immense use and save dollars down the line.

Part 2 Wireless Net Access

Do you have a big business trip coming up? Are you heading off for a working vacation? In this part, we'll focus on wireless technology on the road.

You'll not only find out which wireless standards and equipment will benefit you, but how best to use them. We'll even look at some technologies you should avoid. And so you don't lose your connection on the road, we'll tell you what to bring and who to call if things go south.

Chapter 6

Gearing Up for Wireless on the Move

In This Chapter

- ◆ Technologies that keep you connected
- ◆ Web sites that can keep you online
- ◆ How to send e-mail wirelessly
- ◆ Tools every road warrior should carry

Staying connected to the Net while you travel should be more fun (think working vacation) and less hassle (think roadside breakdown). In this chapter we look at services and technologies that will make your next trip less of a hassle and enable you to get to work—or finish your work and goof off. It's your choice.

It can be confusing with all the standards and technologies available to you. Is *GSM* your sort of technology or is *CDPD* more your style? You won't know until you shop around a bit, and, of course, reading this chapter first can't hurt.

Well-Connected Words

GSM (global system for mobile communications) is used by most of the rest of the world outside the United States, and GSM (PCS 1900) is the digital cellular standard in Europe. CDPD (cellular digital packet data) is a digital wireless network used to transmit data at a maximum rate of 19.2kbps. Most wireless modems use CDPD to connect to the Internet.

Let's consider for a moment, too, that not everyone is so well connected and wireless-savvy as you (or as you will be, after you figure out what CDPD is). For those times when only a fax will do, we look at ways to fax from your mobile devices.

And because you should expect the unexpected, you might want to stock up on some handy tools before you travel. You'll see how to build a mobile toolkit that can help keep you online, on the road, even if it means connecting through a phone jack.

Technology to Go

Let's take a look at your next trip. You're planning on hitting the road and staying in touch with the boss. You'll likely be sending e-mails and checking the Web over one of several networks, and depending on how many devices you carry, communicating using several different technologies.

Any of a number of two-way data networks can handle the tasks. Here are some of the most common, acronym-heavy network types you'll come across when you shop for a wireless phone, PDA, two-way pager, or modem. For the most part, these wireless standards are transparent to you. And the device you choose, or the service provider you prefer, might dictate the type of network over which data is transmitted. That is, you're less likely to pick the technology, than the technology is likely to pick you. But when you start your research, you will probably see these terms, and now you'll know what they mean:

◆ **CDPD (cellular digital packet data).** CDPD is a digital network for wireless data and voice (see Figure 6.1). Many wireless modems use CDPD to transmit data over the Internet at a maximum rate of 19.2kbps. You can purchase a CDPD PC Card modem from a handful of manufacturers, which you can add to your laptop or handheld organizer.

Figure 6.1

The Novatel Merlin is a CDPD modem that fits into the PC Card slot of a laptop.

◆ **GSM (global system for mobile communications).** Used by most of the rest of the world outside the United States, GSM is the digital cellular standard in Europe. You can add a GSM PC Card modem to a laptop or a GSM expansion module to a PDA. GSM transmits data at 9.6kbps. You can also connect your GSM phone to your laptop using a special cable from your service provider. (Voicestream, for example, uses a GSM network, and sells a cable for connecting to your notebook.) You can use GSM in the United States and abroad, but check with your service provider to see what sort of international roaming options you can expect. Don't leave Städte without it.

◆ **CDMA (code division multiple access).** CDMA is digital cellular technology for transmitting voice and data. Next generation CDMA networks, also known as transmits data at a maximum of 153.6kbps. You can connect a CDMA mobile phone to a laptop or PDA. Kyocera and Samsung both make phones that are also Palm OS-based organizers and can be used over a CDMA network.

◆ **GPRS (general packet radio service).** This digital cellular phone standard, currently in limited use in metropolitan areas, is an update to the GSM system that can send and receive data at a speed between 56 and 114kbps.

◆ **TDMA (time division multiple access).** TDMA can carry three times the capacity of analog cellular. Note, however, that North American TDMA as installed by AT&T Wireless cannot carry data.

◆ **Mobitex.** This data-only network is used for two-way wireless communication. Some handheld devices run on the Mobitex network. The RIM BlackBerry and Palm VII both use Mobitex technology.

◆ **Motient.** Like Mobitex, this is a data-only network. Motient says it offers BlackBerry service to 99 percent of the most populated cities in the United States.

◆ **iDEN (integrated digital enhanced network).** Used by Motorola phones for voice and fax transmission. You can also connect an iDEN phone to a laptop with a data cable for Internet access at 9.6kbps. Nextel provides monthly service for iDEN phones.

◆ **AMPS (advanced mobile phone service).** The analog standard for cell phones, used since 1983.

Staying Connected on the Road

No one needs to tell you it's tough on the road. When you want to check your e-mail, you can't get a connection. When you get a connection, you're going into a meeting and can't use it. Road warrior, your pain is felt.

Before you go on the road, take a look at these services and add-ons that can make your PDA or phone more useful and effective. Check out these providers on the Web. They might be able to help you stay in touch, even if you don't have a wireless connection.

◆ **AvantGo (www.avantgo.com).** This is a service that lets you synch up with a Palm OS handheld or Pocket PC, older Windows CE devices, and WAP-enabled phones. After you're synched up, you can then view Web sites offline (you can also synch up in real-time, wirelessly). That's pretty handy when you're on the subway, and the bars that show your signal strength are missing. AvantGo is a particularly helpful service if you need to grab some not-terribly-date-sensitive information. AvantGo also helps Palm OS handhelds connect to Lotus Notes.

◆ **OmniSky (www.omnisky.com).** Wireless services provider OmniSky provides nationwide Internet access for handhelds through wireless modems you can purchase from a handful of manufacturers.

- **GoAmerica (www.goamerica.com).** GoAmerica sells wireless Internet access for two-way pagers and modems for laptops and PDAs. The company also has a monthly service that allows you to view, edit, and fax attachments (including Microsoft Office files) on handhelds with wireless access.

- **Go2 (www.go2.com).** Go2 Online is a great portal service that can help you quickly find restaurants, movie times, and, thankfully, directions, over a handheld (including RIM BlackBerry handhelds). If you access the service using a Sprint PCS mobile phone, Go2 even dials for you the phone number of businesses it helps you locate.

> **Synch Up**
>
> A few simple tricks can mean precious moments of juice on the road. If you don't need sound and can turn it off, do so. Also, consider removing PC Cards when they're not in use. Even when the notebook isn't accessing these cards, they drain battery power. You can also lower the monitor resolution and reduce brightness on your monitor to save power.

Sending E-Mail on the Go

Sending wireless e-mail from your phone or PDA can be simple. The process is nearly identical to sending mail using your computer at home or the office. You just need to know how to start your mail program (check the instructions that came with your wireless device). And if you're using a PDA, you'll need a wireless modem.

Here's how to send e-mail wirelessly from a smart phone or PDA:

1. Launch your e-mail application (see Figure 6.2).

Figure 6.2

Many digital phones offer the ability to send e-mail with just a few clicks.

2. Select the new message text or icon.
3. Address your e-mail.

4. Enter the text in the body of your e-mail.

5. On a phone, select the OK button to send the message.

My phone says OK. Yours may say Yes or Send or something similar. Or you may just use one of the buttons below the display, if the screen prompts you to do so. A PDA will display a Send button to tap with your stylus (see Figure 6.3).

Figure 6.3

E-mailing from a PDA (if it has a wireless modem) is quite simple. It's not much different than e-mailing from a desktop computer.

Well-Connected Words

SMS (short messaging system) is a means of sending short messages, usually no more than 160 characters, using a mobile phone. Messages are stored, so you don't have to keep your phone on to receive them.

If you have a WAP browser on your phone, you can connect to portal services first to send mail. For instance, many phones offer access to the Yahoo! WAP site (see Figure 6.4), and Sprint PCS lets AOL members send mail directly from their phones. And if you just want to send a quick note, your phone may offer *SMS (short messaging system)* service.

Figure 6.4

You can log on to a portal sit, such as Yahoo! if your phone has a WAP browser. From there you can send quick e-mails to pals and co-workers.

Savvy Shopper: Buying Before You Go

It's 2 A.M. when you bolt upright in your hotel bed. This recurring dream is terrible: A dead laptop battery is putting the kibosh on a key PowerPoint presentation.

No need to fear. You can get a new battery, or a range of other accessories, right off the Web. Of course, it's better if you can do the legwork before you go …

- ◆ **iGo (www.igo.com).** iGo is one of the best-known sites for loading up on equipment for your next trip. If it's useful for going mobile, they've probably got it. iGo offers a good selection of wireless phones and PDAs as well as laptop accessories, including batteries (see Figure 6.5).

Figure 6.5

You can find a replacement cradle at iGo.com.

◆ **MobilePlanet (www.mobileplanet.com).** MobilePlanet offers a wide selection of both wireless networking equipment and mobile wireless electronics.

◆ **Road Warrior (www.roadwarrior.com).** Lost your battery? Cat ate your AC Adapter? Check out Road Warrior for wireless travel gear, including accessories for handhelds, laptops, and cellular phones.

◆ **Pricewatch (www.pricewatch.com).** After you've checked out all the other sites, head over to www.pricewatch.com. There you can get the latest products sorted by price in this well-designed and underused site.

> **Synch Up**
>
> You can never get enough battery power on your laptop when traveling. And that low-power warning sound always starts just as you're about put the finishing touches on an important project. Here's how to save a little battery life. Try turning off the AutoSave feature on your office suite applications, such as Microsoft Excel and Word. This allows your hard drive to power down without having to start up again for the AutoSave.

A Mobile Toolkit: Wireless Accessories

In the movies, a doctor shows up in times of crisis with a black kit. The black kit has tools that can mean the difference between life and death. For mobile workers, the kit you pack for yourself is less exciting, but it's still pretty useful.

So what sort of gadgets should you take with you when you travel? The following list shows some tools for connecting wirelessly, and some for backing up your wireless connection.

◆ **A copy of your operating system.** If you need to reinstall a modem, or set up new wireless gear, you might be prompted for files that are on your OS disk. Make sure you have it handy.

◆ **A modem line tester.** In case you can't get a wireless connection on your laptop or PDA, you can still protect your wired, analog modem. Digital phone lines in businesses and hotels can cause damage to a modem. Make sure yours isn't a casualty. You can pick up one of these devices, from IBM (www.ibm.com) or Radio Shack (www.radioshack. com), for about $20.

- **Tweezers.** If you need to pull a phone plug out from under a phone, you'll thank yourself later for these helpful grooming—and dial-up networking—tools.

- **Cigarette lighter attachment.** When you can't get 120-volt AC power on the road, you'll be glad to have a cigarette/airline lighter attachment. You can also purchase a power inverter, for less than $40, that provides AC power to just about any of your handheld electronics. Bonus on-the-road juice tip: If you're traveling internationally, remember to take both power-outlet and phone-jack adapters.

Where to from Here?

Now that you have some background on the types of equipment you can use on the road, it's a good time to consider the nitty-gritty of how to get connected. Each of the next chapters help you find the devices and services that are right for you, in greater detail.

In Chapter 9, "Ring Up the Web," we'll look at both hardware you can use to surf the Internet, and the Internet service providers (ISPs) through which you get access.

The Least You Need to Know

- A range of wireless networks can help you establish Internet connections on the road. The device you choose, such as a phone or PDA, and the service plan you purchase will help make the decision for you.

- A number of Web sites can help you work on the Web, even if you can't get a connection.

- Sending an e-mail using a wireless device is very similar to sending mail at your home computer. If you have a PDA, you'll need a wireless modem to send e-mail (unless your PDA has a wireless modem, as with the Palm VII).

- When your equipment fails you, hop on the Web any way you can, and use the sites we've suggested to find the tools you need to power up again.

- A wireless worker should have a few tools of the trade. From powering up on the road to getting a modem connection at your hotel when your wireless modem won't work, this kit will keep you online. In a word: tweezers.

Staying Connected on the Go

In This Chapter

- ♦ An introduction to frugal wireless connectivity
- ♦ WAP browsing vs. Web browsing
- ♦ When to go wireless
- ♦ Tips for maintaining your connection

Once you have wireless Internet access it's hard to imagine traveling without it. Of course, connecting isn't always a cakewalk. You might have problems finding access, a strong signal, or electricity. Now we'll look at some common pitfalls and how to avoid them.

As with most technologies, a little planning will go a long way. Signing up for a free, Web-based e-mail service might help you stay in touch. And something as simple as e-mailing yourself an important document before you leave could save you trouble down the line.

Here we'll look at some hi-tech and low-tech ways to stay connected on the road. Along the way, I'll mention some tips that can save you time, money, and headaches.

Staying Connected on a Budget

We've talked a bit about the need to find the right device for your needs. Here we get into what I consider frugal wireless computing. If your friends say you're "careful with money," or simply "cheap," then this section, my thrifty friend, is for you.

Wireless technology is cutting edge, true, but it doesn't have to cost an arm and a leg. Doing your work from a sidewalk café is great. Doing it cheaply scores more points.

Here are a few strategies for saving cash on wireless Net access:

◆ If you're in the market for a laptop, first ask yourself how often you'll really need to work on files from the road. If your communications needs are limited to e-mail and light Internet access, you could spend half the cost of a new laptop on a BlackBerry two-way pager (around $400 to $500 for the handheld pager, and $40 a month for unlimited service).

◆ Keep in mind, too, that some wireless Net access devices come at a smaller cost, up-front. A wireless service provider is more likely to charge less for a phone than a wireless modem. A wireless modem for a laptop might cost you between $150 and $400, while older digital phones are nearly given away. Note that wireless Internet access for a digital phone might be charged *in addition* to voice service, and pricing plans can be quite confusing (see Chapter 9, "Ring Up the Web," for more on choosing a wireless Internet service provider).

◆ Use the fewest number of accounts necessary for Internet on the road. You can get Internet access for a Palm handheld by connecting the infrared port to a two-way pager (such as those from SkyTel). Some phones (such as the GSM models from VoiceStream Wireless) allow a similar infrared arrangement with PocketPCs (such as the Compaq iPaq) for Web surfing wirelessly.

CAUTION

Watch Out!

Laptops are a thief's dream, because they're expensive and portable. If you have laptops at work that are stored together (especially if they're checked in and out) keep them in a locked closet, and make sure there are no false ceilings. Keep up on your inventory checks and engrave each unit with your company name and the laptop's ID number.

WAP Your Head Around This: Browse on the Run

Wireless Internet surfing on a mobile phone is dramatically different than what you're used to seeing with the browser on your desktop computer. *WAP (wireless application protocol)* browsing is a more streamlined experience than Web browsing, but if you need to get news and e-mail on the run, you'll find this technology very handy and easy to use (see Figure 7.1).

Well-Connected Words

WAP (wireless application protocol) is the protocol used to provide Internet access, such as web browsing and e-mail, on many mobile phones. Wireless Markup Language (WML) is the language used to create web pages for WAP browsers.

Figure 7.1

Browsing the WAP version of the CBS SportsLine.com site.

Web browsers, such as Netscape and Internet Explorer, read HTML (Hypertext Markup Language), the common language of the Web. HTML pages can be converted to WAP pages, either by hand or using a conversion program. WML allows pages to be linked together, but leaves out graphics and advertisements, increasing the speed in which you can access the information you're looking for.

Note that not all smart phones use WAP browsers. Your service provider might use its own proprietary technology to access information on the Internet. You'll still be able to view Internet information that the service provider has selected. But you need a WAP-enabled phone to view WAP pages.

Dry Run: Testing Before You Go

How can you find out if you're going to be able to stay in touch until you make a test run? In the Navy, it's called a shakedown cruise, and it can be useful for wireless landlubbers.

Take a quick trip with everything you need to work wirelessly, and see where the chips fall. If you come across a mobile phone that barely connects outside the heart of the city or a laptop battery that dies half an hour into an important project, you've got time to fix the problems before your next business trip.

Try the following:

◆ Spend the night somewhere, and use your phone, modem, or pager to connect to the Internet.

◆ Work on an important document and send it back to yourself.

◆ See if you remembered to plug in your batteries the night before.

◆ Send a message with your two-way pager and make sure it arrives.

If any of your wireless devices let you down, give them the old heave-ho.

Synch Up

Most smart phones offer you a new e-mail address. But what if you want to pick up messages from your existing e-mail account? Consider LetsTalk.com's Wireless Inbox (letstalk.wirelessinbox.com), which lets you configure your POP3 (the most common) dial-up mail account at their Web site, and then pick up mail on your phone. You can even send back pre-written responses that you type in at the LetsTalk.com Web page. From your phone, you press a number key to choose the response. Note that an increasing number of wireless providers (Verizon Wireless, Sprint PCS, AT&T Wireless) may already provide a service like this.

Five Common Wireless Oversights

Sometimes staying connected comes down to this: One thing forgotten can offset ten remembered. Your laptop becomes a seven-pound doorstop if you forget the power cable or leave your backup batteries at home.

These mistakes are common, and they can be showstoppers. When you take the time to work out the following simple kinks, you're rewarded with pain-free business trips.

◆ **Lugging around too many devices.** Let's see. You need your cell phone, laptop, PDA, and a two-way pager clipped to your belt. Let's be honest, it's time to slim down. Your mobile phone could replace your PDA or laptop for a short trip. A BlackBerry handheld pager is increasingly replacing laptops for e-mail and messaging. If you don't need to edit content on the road, a two-way pager or smart phone could be your best bet to lighten up.

◆ **Leaving an important document at home.** You arrive at your hotel tired and out of sorts. After checking e-mail on your phone, you fire up the laptop and see the project file you need most is back at the office. Make sure to e-mail or beam the files you're currently working on as well as a few you use frequently, but might not remember, such as a contact list or notes from a meeting. Before you leave, synch up your laptop and desktop. And if you have time, forward important documents before you leave, and check to make sure they arrive before you do.

◆ **Dead batteries.** A classic. You remembered everything except to charge the batteries. What else is there to say? You can't connect wirelessly or do anything else with a lifeless handheld or laptop. Always charge up the night before. So easy to do, and so easy to forget.

◆ **Taking the wrong adapter.** Before you go, make a trip to the local electronics store to pick up any adapter you might need. If you think you might have trouble getting electricity (see the preceding mistake), take along a power inverter. These devices cost less than $40 and provide you with juice on the road. You can plug your laptop, phone, or PDA into any DC cigarette lighter land be up and running.

◆ **Taking wireless when you could go wired.** Wireless has its advantages, but you can't count on getting good clear signals wherever you go. Make sure your analog modem is with you, and dial your ISP with a calling card to avoid outrageous phone bills when you get home.

For quick backups while traveling, you might already have the tools you need to protect your data. E-mail yourself documents to create quick copies.

And consider sending word-processing files that don't need fancy formatting as plain text or Rich Text Format (.rtf). Where possible, it's always a good idea to use text or .rtf format files when trading documents with co-workers, because they reduce the risk of giving and getting macro viruses. Last, if you use a recent version of Microsoft Office, consider setting up Web Folders that save documents online. If you have a dial-up Internet connection, your service provider likely offers 5MB or more of free Web space. Even if you are using the space for a Web site, don't let the excess go to waste. When others bemoan their lost data in times of crisis, you'll be sitting pretty.

Wired or Wireless?

In the last section, we talked about going wireless when wired will do. Despite favoring wireless technology in most cases, there are times when it just makes more sense, and is simpler and less costly, to plug in to a landline.

Until wireless technology is more prevalent, and strong signal strength ubiquitous, you have to make the choice depending on your situation. Here are some examples.

Go wireless when:

- Tying up a phone line isn't an option.
- A wireless connection is the only way to get broadband (as in a hotel or airport with wireless network access).
- You only need text e-mail, and you own a small two-way paging device, mobile phone, or handheld. Everything else can wait until you get back to the office.
- The cost of a phone call on the road outweighs the trouble of plugging in.
- You're traveling in a metropolitan area, and your wireless connection is consistently strong.
- You can't get a wired connection, or you're in a hurry.

Go wired when:

- You have a laptop with an analog, 56kbps modem, and can dial up your ISP for free.

- You need to send an e-mail attachment and bandwidth less than 56kbps just won't cut it.

- Your mobile phone is roaming. (Besides the additional cost of roaming charges, some smart phones won't connect to the Internet when roaming.)

- You have access to an Ethernet network and the hardware to connect.

Synch Up

If you use a PDA or smart phone for Web browsing, you know what a pain it is to jump from site to site. Enter Shadowpack (www.shadowpack.com), a free service that helps you consolidate Web information you're likely to use while traveling. The service works with any device that has a Wireless Access Protocol (WAP) browser. You can use Shadowpack to check weather, news, sports scores, and shop online, among many other uses. And the service makes these tasks easier by adding phone and PDA-friendly menu commands, so navigating the sometimes-underwhelming wireless Web is a little less difficult.

Five Tips for Staying Connected

Your next trip is going to be a doozy. When will you have a good connection to the Internet? A better question might be: When will you be able to get a wireless connection? You've got downtime at the airport, in a cab, at the hotel, in a conference, and at offsite meetings. You need help.

Fear not. Follow these wireless tips and your friends are bound to say that you're the most well-connected person they know:

- Use a co-worker's account in case you can't get online. But get the sign-up information before you go.

- Your PDA or phone's e-mail address might be different than your primary e-mail account. If so, pick up your mail on the Web. Services mentioned in this chapter, such as Wireless Inbox, mentioned earlier, enable you to pick up your mail using a WAP browser.

- Alternatively, use your e-mail program to redirect mail to your PDA or phone. Set up a filter in your e-mail program to forward mail to your handheld, but select options to leave behind attachments.

◆ Check airport and hotel wireless connection availability before you go.

Bet You Didn't Know

Mobile phones continue to drop in price, and that's the way to go, according to New Jersey start-up Dieceland Technologies (www.dtcproducts.com). The company is working on a (very) cheap phone, made of, no kidding, paper. The phone is disposable and costs about $10.

◆ Be flexible about where you connect. It goes without saying that checking mail outside of metropolitan areas is difficult. But obstructions, including walls, trees, and buildings, can hurt your connection. If you have a good signal and a couple minutes, you should check your mail, and then respond when you have a good connection again. To improve your chances for a good signal, keep your antenna vertical and *stand still*. Don't wait to get back to your hotel room to find that it's a well-appointed room with no visible signal.

The Least You Need to Know

◆ On your next trip, consider taking a two-way pager or smart phone instead of lugging around a laptop.

◆ You can use Web site services to make your wireless devices more useful when you travel.

◆ Try before you travel: Check the status of your Internet connectivity in real-world situations, before you leave.

◆ Take steps so that dead batteries, lack of electricity, and a weak signal on your wireless phone or modem doesn't leave you hanging.

Chapter 8

Choosing a Handheld

In This Chapter

- ◆ Checking out Palm OS handhelds
- ◆ Putting a PC in your pocket
- ◆ Options vs. expense
- ◆ Other contenders?

So you've decided to take the plunge. No more slips of paper on your desk with phone numbers. You can give your day runner to the junior partner. Today you get organized.

Well, not so fast. You can spend anywhere from $100 to just less than $1,000 on a PDA, depending on the features you want. Will it be a brilliant color screen or pragmatic monochrome?

First we consider Palm or other Palm-OS based devices. Palm licenses its operating system to other manufacturers, which is why you'll see the familiar Palm icons and buttons on the Sony CLIE and the Handspring Visor (among others).

You might, instead, prefer the comfortably familiar interface of a Windows-based handheld. A more PC-friendly approach could be the Microsoft Pocket PC, which offers the same look and feel (and some of the applications) of a desktop PC.

In this chapter we'll look at the ins and outs of these handhelds, and others, which can help you hit the road without lugging around a laptop.

High Five: Palm OS Devices

Choosing a Palm used to be easy. You came, you bought the Pilot, you left. End of story. Now Palm offers a range of models for different needs. Some are more focused on staying online, browsing, and checking e-mail. Others offer inexpensive means to stay organized on the road.

Of course, by the time you read this book, the models will be different. But the choices will still be the same. Should you spend the money for more memory? Go with color at the expense of battery life? Connect wirelessly, or plug in at home? The decisions you make now help you find a good road companion.

All the Palm OS handhelds, including those made by Handspring, Handera, Sony, and Symbol, provide you with the following features:

- Date book
- To-do list
- Address book
- Memo pad
- Calculator

And of course, they offer the ability to compose and read e-mail. You might send and receive e-mail wirelessly, if you have a built-in modem (as with the Palm VII); you can also connect a Palm OS handheld to an external modem.

Synch Up

Are you interested in a Palm device for Internet browsing? First, check out Palm's wireless Web site at my.palm.com. You can read up on the available services, find out which models work wirelessly, and read about some of the hundreds of sites that are accessible using a Palm handheld. You can sign up for a free MyPalm account, even if you don't own a PDA, for storing your schedule and contact information online.

Handspring

For many people, the obvious handheld choice is a Handspring Visor (see Figure 8.1). These PDAs are reasonably priced, come in cool iMac-like colors, and can work with lots of add-ons.

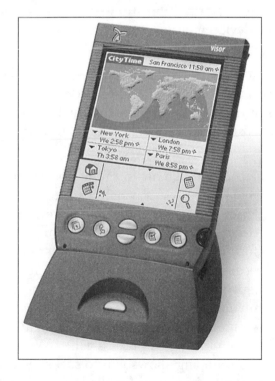

Figure 8.1

A Handspring Visor, ready to synch.

(Photo courtesy of Compaq)

Visors use the Palm operating system, which makes them easy to use and familiar to old Palm hands. Most of the applications you can download and install for the Palm also work with the Handspring.

One of the defining characteristics of the Visor is its expandability: You can add expansion modules to a Visor that offer all sorts of wireless and nonwireless features. You can add a wireless or wired modem, a wireless network card, or a GPS device for finding your way around. You can add phone modules that tie directly into the Visors address book without any setup or installation necessary. And there's even a module for turning the Visor into a cordless phone for chatting into your PDA around the house.

A handful of companies makes wireless modems for the Handspring Visor, but they aren't cheap. You can find and purchase expansion modules at www. handspring.com.

A Palm in the Hand …

Despite competition from young upstarts, Palm still makes some of the most respected PDAs available. The device appeals to many folks as an innovative and expandable wireless companion.

Part of its appeal is that Microsoft doesn't make the device. For those who want a different operating system on their handheld than on their home PC, the intuitive Palm might be just the way to go. Importantly, Palm devices can synchronize data with both PCs and Macs, unlike PC-only, Pocket PCs from Microsoft.

One of the few PDAs on the market with a built-in radio modem, the Palm VII is a sleek way to stay connected when you travel. This Internet-ready device uses a two-way data network called Mobitex that's operated by Cingular Interactive (formerly BellSouth Wireless Data) to send and receive e-mail. Like two-way paging devices, the network is "always-on," so there's no dialing in to your service provider, as you do with an analog modem. The Palm VII offers limited web surfing through a process called Web-clipping. Web clipping allows you to surf sites that are specially developed for the Palm OS and leave most graphics and other nonessential information out of the process to make the most of the limited bandwidth on the Mobitex network.

Watch Out!

Before you purchase a handheld with a color screen, ask two questions. How long is the battery life compared to a similarly configured PDA with a monochrome screen? Often, color screens eat up battery power faster than monochrome ones. And ask yourself whether you really need color, because most color models tend to cost more than their monochrome counterparts.

The line of Palms has been expanded to include models that accept expansion cards, such as the M500 series. Inexpensive models, such as the M100, offer less memory and monochrome screen to cut costs.

Of course, some Palms don't have expansion slots, but you can still add peripherals. You can attach a GPS device, a keyboard, or a modem, for example, to the peripheral connector on the PDA's base.

Other Palm Handhelds

Palm and Handspring make the widest range of Palm OS handhelds, but there are other vendors with very impressive alternatives.

Sony, known for top-quality electronics, makes the multimedia-friendly CLIE (see Figure 8.2). The device offers the ability to play MP3 audio files, and includes headphones for listening. The CLIE is also known for its top-notch color screen.

Figure 8.2

The Sony CLIE PDA.

(Photo courtesy of Sony Electronics, Inc.)

The CLIE is quite expandable. Its proprietary Memory Stick cards enable you to add 8MB of removable storage. That said, many MP3 audio files are several megabytes or more, which eats up Memory Sticks at a pretty quick clip. And, the concept of downloading MP3s wirelessly, over anything less than a broadband connection, makes for tough going.

As for wireless Internet use, options are fairly limited. A CLIE with an IR port might be able to connect to a wireless phone for Internet access. Check the Sony Web site (www.sony.com) regarding compatibility with your phone.

You can also purchase a Sony analog (wired) modem, which clips on for e-mail use and browsing the Web. A wireless PC modem is available for CDPD networks.

Thankfully, the CLIE (like most Palm devices) offers synching with the Macintosh, though you might need to purchase additional software to do so.

Take a PC: Windows Handhelds

The Windows-based Pocket PC operating system is becoming an increasingly popular way to go wireless. A handful of companies employ the Pocket PC operating system, increasing your chances of finding a reasonably priced system with a good bit of power, a great-looking color screen, and loads of memory.

Pocket PCs all offer some sort of expansion capability, so you can insert a PC Card, in some models, to connect by modem, or attach a cable to your mobile phone and wirelessly dial up an Internet service provider (ISP).

Some of the Pocket PCs now offer many wireless capabilities. The Compaq iPaq is a good example (see Figure 8.3), as you can purchase it with add-ons that enable you to insert a wireless PC Card modem or wireless network card that enable you to hop onto an 802.11b (Wi-Fi) wireless network.

Well-Connected Words

To connect a handheld device for synching to a computer, a **cradle** is a sort of docking station for your PDA. Most cradles offer both AC power (for charging batteries) and a serial or USB connection to the computer for downloading Web pages to read offline, synching e-mail, and updating contact lists and calendars, among other functions.

Another handy wireless Pocket PC trick is the ability to connect wirelessly via an infrared port to some cell phones, allowing the two devices to work together and provide you with Internet access.

All Pocket PCs, including the Casio Cassiopeia and the Hewlett-Packard Jornada, come with a slimmed down version of Microsoft's Internet Explorer for browsing the Web. The browser offers both text and graphics, and most Pocket PCs offer sharp color screens.

If you use the Pocket PC's version of Outlook, you can send and receive mail, and then synch up the inbox on your PDA and desktop or laptop computer using a *cradle*.

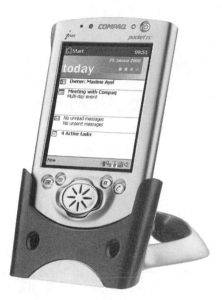

Figure 8.3

Compaq iPaq and cradle.

(Photo courtesy of Compaq)

Other Contenders

Competitors for your PDA dollar are, sadly, few at this time.

Handheld-computer maker Psion makes the Revo, a popular device with a clamshell design and keyboard. The Diamond Mako, a Psion handheld sold by Sonicblue, was a well-received budget PDA based on the Revo design. It was unfortunately discontinued after Psion focused on areas other than the consumer market. You might still see this handy wireless PDA on eBay or other auction sites.

Synch Up

If you choose to buy a Palm that doesn't have built-in Internet access, you can purchase the Mobile Internet Kit. You can connect to your phone by infrared, if your phone has a port, or connect the Palm to a cable. If this sounds attractive, check Palm's Web site (www.palm.com) to see if your phone is compatible.

Other handhelds, such as the Sharp Zaurus and Xircom Rex, have also been discontinued. They were primarily meant to be used for contact management and organizing. Although they can synch up to a PC, they're not used for wireless e-mail and browsing.

The PDA market turns on a dime, so your best option is to find a model that has the features you need and, importantly, some staying power. Pick a manufacturer with good word of mouth. The Palm OS and Pocket PCs are all good bets.

A more likely candidate, if you're not impressed with current wireless PDA offerings, is a mininotebook. Made by big guns such as IBM and NEC, these lighter than laptop devices have full-size keyboards, and expansion options similar to a regular laptop. Mininotebooks sometimes use a full-featured operating system such as Windows 2000, or they might use a portable version, such as Windows CE.

Synch Up

Want Windows to go? Windows CE is the miniature version of Windows for PDAs. The current version, 3.0, is most-often called the Pocket PC operating system. Handheld PCs (devices with larger screens, and sometimes, a keyboard) are targeted at enterprise users. Handheld PCs use a version of Windows CE, too. The Windows CE operating system includes scaled-down (or "pocket") versions of Microsoft Word, Excel, Outlook, and PowerPoint; some models include the database program Access. Some argue that the Palm OS is simpler because it doesn't rely on a Windows-based menu system and gets the job done more quickly. Others prefer the familiar Windows interface and applications. We look at making Palm handhelds and Pocket PCs talk to each other in Chapter 17, "Beaming with Pride," in the "Making Friends: Pocket PCs and Palm Handhelds" section.

General Concerns

Regardless of whether you purchase a Pocket PC, Palm OS handheld, or a device with a proprietary OS, there are a number of features you might consider adding as "must-haves" on your shopping list.

Handhelds are many and varied, but these features in the sections that follow are common to most of them (and come at a cost).

Can You Expand?

Just about every PDA provides some sort of way to add peripherals, such as wireless modems and network cards. Some require additional add-ons for your, er … add-ons. The Compaq iPaq, requires that you insert a PC Card expansion jacket, for instance, before you can insert a PC Card device, such as a wireless modem.

If you're considering purchasing a particular model, check that vendor's Web site to see what sort of expansion capabilities that PDA has. The Palm OS and Pocket PCs offer more expansion capabilities than other PDAs. And even within those categories, some models offer more expansion options than others.

Make sure your PDA is widely supported by companies that make peripherals for your model. The Sony CLIE, for example, has fewer add-on options than any of the Handspring Visors.

Color or Monochrome

If you plan to download photos and videos to your PDA, you probably want a color screen. Let's just say that pictures in monochrome don't make your wireless PDA feel very futuristic.

If you need a PDA for quick e-mails and contact management, the savings of a monochrome display outweigh the benefits. Color comes at a cost, in more ways than one: A color PDA is more expensive, and the screen is more demanding on batteries.

Battery life is key, obviously. If your PDA can't make it out to lunch with you, its wireless Web features won't do you much good. Many PDAs use standard batteries (AA, AAA) that can be replaced every few weeks or so, rather than recharged.

Wireless Web

You want to know what sort of Web browsing is available with your PDA. Can you view most Web sites using a particular model? Can you get text *and* graphics?

Some PDAs limit the Web sites that can be viewed to ones that have been optimized

Well-Connected Words

Web clipping is a way of displaying information from the Web on the small screen of a phone or PDA. The Palm VII uses Web clipping to request information, such as a stock quote or bank balance, minus the graphics, from Internet sites over wireless connections. The Palm VII series PDAs are ready to hit the Internet, out of the box, as soon as you activate the Palm.Net wireless Internet service.

for that particular PDA. Find out how many sites you can visit and if they need to be specially constructed to be read by your handheld. WAP sites cannot be read by phones without WAP capability, for instance, and some phones use their own proprietary browsers.

Palm VII PDAs use *Web clipping*. This is a means of extracting the important information from a site and leaving graphics and multimedia behind. It's a limited way of gaining access to information on the Web, but it can be very quick and useful (and if you like, you can download a Web browser to view the Web on your palm). Know what you're getting into before you buy.

The Least You Need to Know

- ◆ Palm OS handhelds provide a handy way to organize information and access the Internet, and they come in a range of devices from a handful of manufacturers.
- ◆ Microsoft's Pocket PCs offer a familiar interface and portable access for e-mail and full Web browsing.
- ◆ Web clipping enables you to pull text-based information quickly from Web sites to view on a Palm VII.
- ◆ No matter what PDA you choose, your options, and added expense includes color or monochrome screens, expandability, and wireless Web access.

Chapter 9

Ring Up the Web

In This Chapter

- ◆ Checking out Web phones
- ◆ Surveying wireless Web phone service providers
- ◆ The flexible wireless modem

So I get a call from my mother-in-law, who's vacationing in Atlantic City. The slots are hot, she says, but she can't send an e-mail to my aunt about her winnings. Her cell phone just isn't up to the task.

Problem is, she's got an older cell phone with no Internet access. I tell her that she should go buy a new phone. Most digital or digital/analog (a.k.a. dual mode) cell phones now offer Internet access.

She could also use a wireless modem. She can keep her old analog cellular phone for voice calls and use the modem to go online. And she can use the wireless modem without tying up her phone line at her hotel (and avoid all those expensive hotel-phone charges).

In this chapter we're going to help you break down exactly what you need for mobile Web access, from the hardware to the service plans to the pesky cables you need to make sure it all runs.

Minibrowsing: Smart Phones

I'll let you in on a secret. Of all the devices discussed in this book, the one I really can't live without is my smart phone.

Some scoff at my phone's small screen and the limited messages I can type with a tiny keypad. But it's the one wirelessly connected device that I use every day:

- It serves as a modem for my laptop (using a serial cable).
- It reminds me of appointments.
- It lets me sign on to the wireless Internet and get news, movie times, and directions on the fly. (Some people even do a little shopping, but I use mine mostly for research before I buy, at sites like edmunds.com, a car-buying guide.)
- My phone's infrared port also lets me connect directly with my PDA for surfing wirelessly. (Not all Web phones can do this—GSM phones are more likely to offer the feature.)

Some phones include a built-in modem, and others require you to install a software modem on your laptop or PDA. Either way, they're incredibly handy road tools. What's the difference between a smart phone and a *cellular* phone? Well, smart phones are cellular, but not every cellular phone is a Web phone.

Well-Connected Words

Mobile phones are sometimes called **cellular,** or cell phones, because the geographic area in which they can send and receive a signal is called a *cell*. A cell phone can be digital (where your voice is converted to 0s and 1s, then compressed) or analog. The analog cell phone standard is called AMPS (Advanced Mobile Phone System). A cell covers a relatively small geographic area. Your carrier's system may cover a large region and include hundreds of cells.

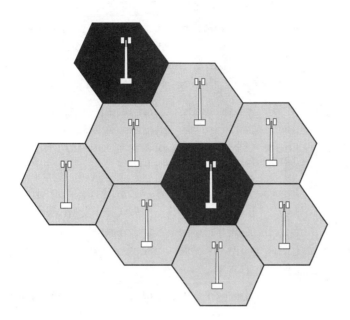

Figure 9.1

A cell covers a relatively small geographic area. Your carrier's system may cover a large region and include several hundreds of cells.

There are two important questions you need to know the answers to when you buy a mobile phone to go online:

◆ **Does the phone have built-in capability to go online?** Many new digital phones offer Internet service, but not all do. Analog phones don't offer most of the features we've come to expect from digital phones, such as access to the Internet, caller ID, and e-mail.

◆ **Can you buy a cable to connect the phone to your laptop or PDA and surf the Web?** If you buy a phone, then later find you can't purchase a cable to connect it to your computer, you're out of luck. See the example of a Web phone connected to a laptop in Figure 9.2.

Figure 9.2

A Web phone connected to a laptop.

(Photo courtesy of Sprint PCS)

How to Choose a Web Phone

If you go to a dinner party, you're likely to see three people, with three different phones, who purchased them in three different ways.

Watch Out!

If you use a Web phone for Internet access, make sure you know if you're eating up the overall monthly minutes included in your plan. If you pay by the minute for Web access, you can often check your usage on your provider's Web site (www.sprintpcs.com, for example).

Perhaps you admire the features and sleek shape of one phone at the party. You could ask about its manufacturer, then choose a wireless phone company that offers service for it.

Maybe you overhear that one partygoer pays a flat fee for wireless Internet access on her phone. That sounds pretty good, you think, and ask who provides her phone service.

Last, you might go online and do a bit of research from both angles. Check into phones you like, and compare them to the best bargains, coupons, and other incentives you can find on the Web.

I lean toward choosing your provider first, one with good coverage in your area. But it's your choice, so let's take a look at the pros and cons of each.

How to Choose a Web Phone: Phone Centric

Maybe you want a phone that fits in your shirt pocket or a small purse. You might want find a phone that when flipped open is both compact and easy to talk on (an important consideration, no?). No matter what your preferences, there's a phone out there that will fit your needs. Some considerations to consider include …

- **Screen size.** For surfing the wireless Web, you probably want a phone that can display more than a few lines of text. Add extra lines, however, and you get a bigger phone, of course. Somewhere you're going to make a tradeoff: Easy on the eyes, or easy to carry.
- **Cost.** You can get phones for free and phones that cost a bundle. A less expensive phone probably goes light on features, such as organizer capabilities, infrared, screen size, a color screen, and short battery life.
- **Connectivity.** Can you connect your phone to your laptop or PDA for surfing, either by infrared port, or through a serial cable?

How to Choose a Web Phone: Provider Centric

Because phone offerings are similar, more likely than not, you'll choose a provider that offers the combination or price, features, and connectivity time you want.

Of course, the number one concern is making sure the provider covers the areas where you live, work, and travel. If you can't get a signal, and you're constantly being charged for *roaming*, you'll use your phone less and less.

You're not just going to be using the phone for surfing the Web. So look for a plan that offers a reasonable policy on roaming, a.k.a. making calls outside of your provider's network, especially if you use an analog or dual-mode phone. Some providers charge separately for long distance and roaming—not good bang for your buck.

Well-Connected Words

When you shop for a digital phone, you will often hear the term **roaming**, which typically incurs a charge determined by your service provider. Roaming occurs when you travel outside your provider's wireless network. Sometimes roaming occurs when you travel away from a digital calling network and use an analog one. A phone that can use both digital and analog networks is often called a dual-mode phone. Here's the catch: The charges associated with roaming are pretty confusing, so make sure you understand how you'll be billed when you sing up for a plan. In some cases there may be charge for voice roaming, but not for data roaming. Definitions of roaming can vary widely—be prepared.

How to Choose a Smart Phone: Comparison-Shopping

Finally, here's a way to take the big picture approach to buying a Web phone. Hop online, and look for Web-based vendors that let you do some comparison-shopping of phone and service provider features before you buy.

Getconnected.com (www.getconnected.com) offers a wide selection of phones and tools for matching your needs and the phone and service providers' offerings (see Figure 9.3). Both Netscape (www.netscape.com) and Yahoo! (www.yahoo.com) offer shopping links that enable you to compare providers and plans. You can also stop in at a local electronics store, such as Circuit City, Best Buy, or any shop that offers multiple phones and multiple plans.

Figure 9.3

*Checking out
GetConnected.com.*

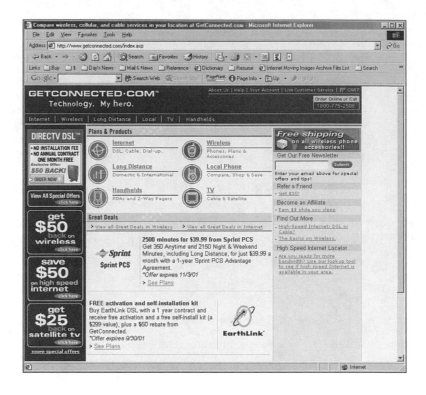

Picking a Smart Phone ISP

Ready to dive in to Web phone service? You might want to pick up your pain reliever of choice before you start researching. To say monthly costs and services vary widely is like saying a shark is kind of dangerous when it's hungry.

For more current information, check out the providers online. Most list local, regional, and national plans that affect coverage areas and monthly charges.

Synch Up

You can take VoiceStream GSM service internationally if you have A GSM phone. And if you don't have the right phone, you can rent one from Voice-Stream. (See the accompanying list.)

Here are some things to consider seriously when deciding on a plan:

- ◆ Check out online coverage maps, and be warned that straying from your provider's service areas can mean big roaming fees ranging from $.39 to nearly a dollar per minute, *plus extra long-distance charges.*

- Keep in mind that you might not be able to access the Web in all areas where voice service is available.

- Providers bundle different features into your packages. Text messaging, personal Web sites, and e-mail address are available and are sometimes included in the plans or offered for a small extra fee.

- You might have to pay an activation fee that usually runs between $10 to $35. If your provider requires a year-long contract (some, such as Sprint, do not) you might be charged a fee if you terminate the contract early.

- Ask a potential provider if Web minutes are billed differently than voice minutes. Some plans offer unlimited surfing, for a set monthly fee. Others subtract the time you surf from your plan's overall minutes after you've paid a Web fee, usually $5 to about $30.

Listed as follows are the major Web phone service providers and some recent pricing. Monthly charges, and promotions, turn on a dime, but this should give you a general idea of what you're getting into.

- **Sprint PCS** (sprintpcs.com)

  Minutes: 40 to 4,000

  Monthly cost: $19.99 to $149.99

  How Internet access is billed: A $5 monthly fee is tacked onto your phone service plan to access the Web. Internet minutes are deducted from your allowed phone minutes.

  Coverage: Sprint PCS coverage is quite extensive, but if you slip into analog roam, you won't be able to access the Internet at all.

Synch Up

Considering a two-way pager (such as the BlackBerry handheld or Motorola's T900)? Service plans range from about $10 to $60 a month. Plans do not typically bill by the minute as Web phones do. The amount of data you can send ranges from 15KB to 3,000KB to unlimited usage. As a rule of thumb, one message runs about 1KB. Providers include GoAmerica (www.goamerica.com), Cingular Wireless (www.cingular.com), Arch Wireless (www.arch.com), WebLink (www.weblinkwireless.com), SkyTel (www.skytel.com), and OmniSky (www.omnisky.com). You are also likely to pay an activation fee of between $20 to $40.

◆ **Cingular Wireless** (www.cingular.com)

Minutes: 30 to 3,000

Monthly cost: $19.99 to $199.99

How Internet access is billed: Cingular has two plans for accessing the Internet with your phone, costing between $6.99 and $21.99. One plan ticks off minutes from your plan, while another allows you to send or receive a certain number of kilobits per month to send or from you phone.

Coverage: Surfing the Internet outside your local digital calling area can incur roaming charges to the tune of $.69 per minute.

◆ **Verizon** (www.verizon.com)

Minutes: 45 to 3,000

Monthly cost: $25 to $300

How Internet access is billed: In addition to your monthly phone service charge, you'll be billed $6.99 to $12.95 for Internet access, which enables you to receive 100 to 600 e-mails (Verizon calls them "alerts").

Coverage: Good coverage in the eastern part of the USA. If you roam west, you'll be charged $.65 per minute.

◆ **AT&T** (attws.com)

Minutes: 60 to 3,000

Monthly cost: $19.99 to $199.99

How Internet access is billed: AT&T calls its Web service PocketNet. You can get the most basic service for free with the purchase of a digital PCS phone, or you can pay between $6.99 and $14.99 for Internet access with features varying. If you surf from your phone, you're billed the standard airtime and roaming, if applicable, and your allowed minutes are depleted. However, if you tie into the Web from your laptop, you'll be charged $.05 per kilobit sent to or from your phone.

Coverage: Roaming charges are $.60 per minute plus $.15 a minute for long distance.

◆ **VoiceStream** (www.voicestream.com)

Minutes: 75 to 2,500

Monthly cost: The VoiceStream plans range from $19.99 to $139.99, but you can only get the Internet option if you purchase DataStream service on top of your VoiceStream package.

How Internet access is billed: DataStream costs $29.99 for 1,500 minutes with $.05 per minute for minutes over your limit.

Coverage: There are some conspicuous state-wide omissions, including California. Roaming costs $.49, plus long-distance charges, but some VoiceStream plans allow you to roam for free.

CAUTION

Watch Out!

Connecting your phone to your laptop for Internet access might cost you more than simply accessing the Internet using your smart phone alone. Some providers distinguish accessing the Internet from you phone and from a laptop. If you hook up with a laptop using your phone as a modem, you might get hit with a "tethering" fee for the amount of data transferred or for minutes spent surfing (as with AT&T). At the very least, minutes might be charged against your allowed phone plan if you use a laptop.

Disconnect: Wireless Modems

In the world of wireless, the utility player is the wireless modem. When you're not sure how to get connected, it's wise to keep in mind that a wireless modem is one of the most adaptable accessories you can add to your laptop or PDA.

If your phone's manufacturer doesn't sell a cable to connect to your PDA or laptop or it doesn't have an infrared port, a wireless modem might be the only way to get your laptop or PDA surfing the Internet cord-free.

A PC Card modem for your PC or Mac is likely to communicate via CDPD at a pokey 14.4kbps. The modem, which usually has a small antenna, included a transceiver, which acts as a radio, connecting to a single network type, and sometimes a single provider. You won't exactly be flying along, but you should be fine to send e-mail and light surfing. Faster speeds are on the way, including the service formerly known as Ricochet, which sends and receives data at up to 128kbps; for now, most folks are surfing wirelessly at sub-19.2kbps speeds.

You can start your search by checking out the trade publications for the latest modem recommendations:

- ◆ www.idg.net
- ◆ www.cnet.com
- ◆ www.techweb.com
- ◆ www.zdnet.com

If you use a PDA, your best bet for finding an appropriate modem is to visit the Web site of the company that makes your handheld, such as:

- ◆ Microsoft (www.pocketpc.com)
- ◆ Palm (www.palm.com)
- ◆ Handspring (www.handspring.com)

Modems: Picking a Provider

If you've decided a wireless modem is the way to go for your handheld or laptop, you need an ISP that offers coverage in the areas where you live and travel. Of the Internet service providers available, GoAmerica (www.goamerica.com) and OmniSky (www.omnisky.com) have the broadest range of offerings.

Modem service will likely run you between $10 and $50 a month, depending on whether you want basic or unlimited service. The modem itself, from manufactures, including Sierra Wireless (www.sierrawireless.com) and Novatel (www.novatel.com), will probably set you back just under $300.

Both providers offer service for wireless modems for the Palm OS and Pocket PCs. They also have service plans for BlackBerry two-way pagers. You can search their sites for the latest prices and offerings.

After you have a modem picked out, you can search for service plans at Connected.com or CNET's wireless site (wireless.cnet.com). Both of these sites include pricing and service information, and you can compare current information on current plans.

The Least You Need to Know

- Web phone service providers vary widely in offerings for the wireless surfer.

- Look out for hidden fees when shopping for a Web phone, including long distance, roaming charges, and "tethering" fees (extra cost for connecting your phone to a laptop).

- Wireless modems are the way to connect if you can't use your phone with your PDA or laptop.

- Consider a service such as GoAmerica or OmniSky can help you find the right modem, network, and computer combination.

Chapter 10

Wireless E-Mail Devices

In This Chapter

◆ Wireless e-mail just about everywhere

◆ What's a BlackBerry?

◆ Talking about two-way paging

◆ Why WAP?

If a laptop seems too weighty to lug around, and a Pocket PC or Palm OS device is more machine than you need, a two-way messaging device might be just the ticket. They're light and relatively inexpensive, and you look cool typing with your thumbs (as you might have guessed, the keyboards are pretty tiny).

What these devices sometimes lack in large screens they often make up with that little keyboard. (Ever try composing e-mails on a PDA without a keyboard? It isn't pretty.)

Of course, you can always go with a mobile phone. You won't have a keyboard, but you won't have to carry another electronic gadget either. Internet-capable smart phones just keep getting smarter—and faster.

E-Mail on the Run

Two-way pagers might not be able to balance a spreadsheet or create a database, but let's be frank, who wants to? Sure, sometimes you might *have to*, but we're talking about something that can handle your e-mail and scheduling tasks without the weight of a laptop.

Bet You Didn't Know

The NHL hockey team in North Carolina, the Hurricanes, sells tickets by wireless Web through Internet-capable phones and PDAs. Fans can even buy Hurricanes-branded PCS phones, with links to Hurricanes and other hockey Web sites. The team plans to add trivia games that can be played during games using smart phones.

Most two-way pagers include some way to download and install small applications. And many also provide the ability to retrieve information from the Internet, connecting to information services that provide data on the fly, such as news and stock quotes. Most offer the ability to set alarms (you can set a two-way pager to vibrate in quiet situations) and manage contact lists, as well.

Because you don't want to be overloaded with noncritical mail on the run, you can take steps to reduce your load. You can set filters for your two-way pager, so that only the really important messages reach you when you're out of the office.

Take It to the RIM

When I was a kid, we didn't have two-way pagers. We had to throw pencils and spitballs to get each other's attention, at considerable risk to ourselves. Now the well-connected teenager, as well as the wireless professional, has a much safer way to make a point.

When we consider mail on the go, the BlackBerry immediately jumps to mind (see Figure 10.1). These very cool and increasingly popular devices provide wireless Net connectivity, both e-mail and text-only Web access, just about anywhere.

Figure 10.1

Compaq sells a wireless RIM two-way pager, the iPAQ BlackBerry W1000, which connects to corporate e-mail accounts and synchronizes calendar information wirelessly.

(Photo courtesy of Compaq Computer Corporation)

Made by Canadian firm Research in Motion (RIM), the BlackBerry transmits data over a paging network. When you send e-mail, a copy arrives in your home e-mail inbox. If someone sends you a message, you get a copy on your BlackBerry in a format that is easy to read on the small screen. You can also keep your PC and BlackBerry handheld up to date by synching the devices using a cradle that connects to the computer.

RIM makes a handful of wireless e-mail handhelds. One line of the devices, the Enterprise models, synch up with Microsoft Outlook or Lotus Notes, enabling you to use your office e-mail on the go. If your office uses Microsoft Exchange, you can even synch up your calendar wirelessly.

Another series of BlackBerry handhelds, the Internet models, provide you with a separate, new e-mail address for checking mail on the go. Service providers (prices and services vary by provider) include Cingular (www.cingular.com), Motient (www.motient.com), EarthLink (www.earthlink.com), and GoAmerica (www.goamerica.com).

Synch Up

One of the hassles of the new wireless age is having too many mailboxes. A selling point of the wireless BlackBerry handhelds is the ability to send and receive mail using your office e-mail address, without anyone knowing you're not at your desk. Although you might not want to get mail from the Big Cheese while you're at the dentist, it opens up new possibilities for staying in touch with co-workers while you catch a day game at the ballpark.

For quick e-mails you might choose a pager-sized BlackBerry handheld (such as the RIM 850 or RIM 950); others have a larger display and are more the size of a PDA (such as the RIM 857 or RIM 957). Each model has a small QWERTY keyboard and a scrolling wheel for making selections from menus.

You can download additional applications, such as a stock quote-checking program, but you might have to pay extra for the added features.

Who's a BlackBerry good for? Anybody who needs e-mail on the run and wouldn't mind trading in a full-featured PDA for something a little smaller, with nearly as much usefulness. Sadly, it's not a good choice for Mac users, as it doesn't yet synch up with those of us who Think Different.

Want to know if BlackBerry is right for you? Check out RIM's BlackBerry site (www.blackberry.net) and follow the links to a service provider. Then see if the area where you live is covered.

Talk Amongst Yourselves

BlackBerry isn't the only two-way messaging device on the block. Priced in the same range and with similar features are the two-way paging devices from Motorola. The company makes a range of text messengers. In this section we look at the devices broadly and address their capabilities (and figure out what they're really good for).

Some of the Motorola two-way pagers, the TimePort and PageWriter, for example, have an infrared port for synching with a PC. These models offer PDA-like features, such as appointment tracking and contact lists.

The Talkabout T900 is a less expensive two-way pager, with a four-line monochrome LCD screen (the other Motorola pagers display nine lines) in your choice of translucent colors. You can use the device to pick up mail at its own address, or you can have mail forwarded to the device. The Talkabout is also often bundled with service from a provider, including AOL and Yahoo! and obviously picks up mail from those accounts.

Because different service providers offer service for the devices, your coverage area might help you decide which model you can use. For additional cost, service plans might include data services, including sports scores, movie times, and news.

For those on a budget, the T900 is the obvious starting place. For a pocket-sized PDA replacement, the TimePort and PageWriter models are a safer bet. Motorola also makes the .V series, which might suit those who want the ability to make phone calls with their paging device. And a cool-looking model called the Accompli 009 (about $600) includes GSM mobile phone features and a headset (see Figure 10.2).

Bet You Didn't Know

Hate the finger mangling associated with sending e-mail on your mobile phone? You can purchase a keyboard that connects to some models. The Motorola iBoard works with the i50sx, i55sr, and i85s and costs just under $100. The full-size keyboard folds up for storage.

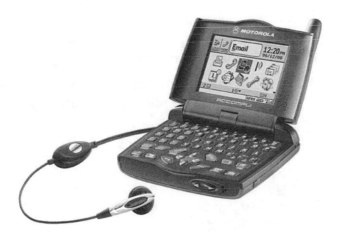

Figure 10.2

The Motorola Accompli 009 is a messaging device that also has mobile phone functions.

(Photo courtesy of Motorola, Inc.)

Phones on the Run

Web phones are, as Yogi Bear would say (if Yogi Bear were a mobile professional), smarter than the average phone. From warning you about a meeting to browsing the Web, you can get a lot of bang for very little buck.

Palm OS phones, like those from Samsung and Kyocera, are some of the neatest—and most expensive—phones around. But until they get smaller, and less expensive, a mobile phone with some Web-browsing and e-mail features meets most folks' budgets. These days, all the major phone vendors sell a model that's Web savvy.

More and more often, you'll have a hard time finding a phone that *doesn't* offer PDA-like features. The choice has more to do with whether the phone supports the current desktop or laptop computer you use. If it doesn't, consider whether the features you like about your phone are worth the hassle of duplicate entries on each device or the trouble it takes to create a workaround and get them on the same page.

Many Web phones offer a limited set of contact and appointment management capabilities. The best of them also connect to your laptop and act as a modem.

Depending on the model you choose, you might also get instant messaging features with a Web phone. IM can be a fun feature, and it's pretty handy on the receiving end, but it can be tricky to type up even short notes. The composing difficulties can be minimized if the phone includes an onscreen virtual keyboard menu and stylus (as some of the most expensive do).

A good smart phone should also include a relatively large screen for Internet (WAP) browsing (but not so large as to make the phone too bulky). Almost any phone should be fine for picking up e-mail.

Obviously, you also want to know how long the Web phone you're considering can hold a charge. And voice quality will make or break a phone—all the PDA features and Web browsing capabilities you can dream of don't make up for a phone that makes you sound like you're calling from the bottom of a pool.

Unfortunately, some good, well-featured, and reasonably priced Web phones are digital only. That's fine for traveling in the city, and that might be all you need, but you want a phone that has both analog and digital service, for greater coverage, when traveling out of metropolitan areas.

All the major carriers, including Sprint PCS, Cingular Wireless, Verizon, AT&T Wireless, and Voicestream Wireless, offer Internet service for smart phones. Pick a model with the features that you know you need, and read up on the voice quality from available reviews and word of mouth. Find a phone with a good mix of these features, and you'll have a roadside companion that makes you think twice about taking a handheld with you.

Choosing a Plan

As Web features become more common in mobile phones, deals keep getting better for service. It's a buyer's market, and the latest/greatest phone from six months back might be a real bargain today, with thousands of minutes at your disposal.

Web access typically costs less than $10 on top of your monthly fees, and it's becoming more common to see the service added at no additional charge.

Tip number one when choosing a plan for your Web phone: Ask a lot of questions. Do your overall monthly minutes include your wireless Web minutes? Will you be charged by file size or the number of characters sent in your plan? Where possible, look for a plan that offers unlimited, all-you-can e-mail pricing.

Checking Out WAP

Because you'll be hitting the Web with your phone, you might want to know a little more about how wireless browsing works. That being the case, a discussion of WAP (wireless application protocol) is in order (see Figure 10.3).

Figure 10.3

Checking out Yahoo! on a WAP phone.

WAP is the language, or protocol, used to transmit data from Web servers to WAP-enabled phones. Keep in mind though, that not all Internet access through the Internet is WAP. Phones are more likely than pagers, or PDAs, to use a WAP browser. Some smart phones use their own proprietary means of accessing data on the Internet.

When you select a link using a WAP-capable device (by pointing with a smart phone's miniature mouse or other selection device), a request is sent using radio waves to your Internet access provider. The provider forwards the request for data to the server with the page you want to see.

The Web site sends the page back and your provider uses a gateway server to convert the code used to create a Web page (HTML) into *WML* (*Wireless Markup Language*), which displays the page, *sans* graphics, on the phone's screen.

Well-Connected Words

WML (Wireless Markup Language) is the language used by Web designers to construct pages, called *cards*, for wireless devices. The language is similar to HTML, which is used to construct World Wide Web pages. If you've ever worked with your own Web pages, you probably can pick up WML pretty easily. Check out www. builder.com for more information on creating your own WML pages.

In Figure 10.4 we see the WAP site for the British newspaper *The Guardian* on the left and the WML code that constructs the page on the right. This program is called Deck-It WML Previewer. If you'd like to see what WAP browsing looks like before purchasing a smart phone, you can download the emulator at www.pyweb.com.

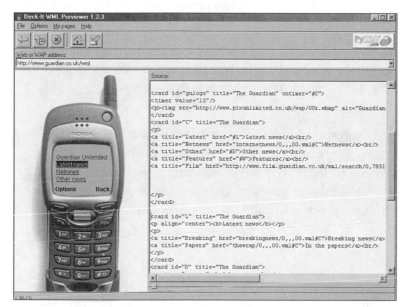

Figure 10.4

Here's a WAP page, viewed with a program, called an emulator, which helps developers check out their pages before they publish them.

Web designers have to create WAP versions of their Web pages, which are sent back to the gateway server, as a normal Web page would be.

Interested in seeing if WAP browsing is for you? WAP emulators are available online, which enables you to see what you're getting into. You can check one out at www.gelon.net, which provides a quick view of how a page looks on different WAP phones.

E-Mail Alone

If you're primarily interested in simply receiving messages, you can choose from a handful of devices that pick up (but don't send) your e-mail.

Well-Connected Words

Wireless narrowband, in contrast to fast-moving wireless broadband, is the name for the monochrome, small-screen Internet access we currently see in mobile phones and two-way pagers. Typically these devices connect at 9.6kbps to 14.4kbps.

One of the most notable devices in this category is the Timex Internet Messenger watch. Timex offers a line of watches that downloads weather, sports scores, flight times, as well as e-mail. The Little LCD screen receives text messages, up to 100 characters long, through a service plan from SkyTel.

You can pick up mail using your existing account, by forwarding the messages from your inbox to the watch (at an address that is yourpagingnumber@timex.skytel.com).

Of course, if you're only interested in receiving mail over a *wireless narrowband* network, most paging providers offer some sort of e-mail forwarding service. (You don't necessarily have to wear your pager on your wrist.) That said, you might find paging-based e-mail services lacking some features you need, such as the ability to pick up mail from multiple e-mail addresses.

What's Next?

The future of e-mail devices looks promising. In particular, access by phone should improve dramatically, as services such as GPRS (General Packet Radio Service) increase the speed of browsing.

Not only will you be able to browse more quickly with GPRS, which is an upgrade to the GSM network, you can make a call while browsing, and your Internet access is always on. That is, you don't have to dial in to get e-mail, and e-mail messages appear as they arrive.

Increased speed will lead, slowly, toward more advanced abilities, such as downloading music and watching video. That said, even the generation of service to follow GPRS called 3G (third generation) is expected to run at a maximum of 128kbps, which is not quite the speed of home broadband technologies such as DSL or cable modems. If you're hoping to watch movies on your phone in the near future, you'd better expect them to be small and choppy. But picking up e-mail and browsing the Web should get easier as service providers roll out faster wireless Internet service.

The Least You Need to Know

◆ BlackBerry handheld pagers enable you to send and receive e-mail wire-lessly. The devices are particularly useful in offices that use Microsoft Outlook and Lotus Notes.

◆ Motorola makes a range of two-way pagers for staying in touch on the go from just about anywhere.

◆ WAP is a way of serving up Web pages so that the small displays on handheld devices can easily read them.

◆ Future wireless Web services should make wireless e-mail devices even more useful, as wireless Internet speeds are beginning to approach those of home broadband services.

Part

Wireless at Home and Work

Got an office that's still walking files across the room on those fiddly floppies? Want to share an Internet connection at every computer in your house without stringing cables through your drywall? We've got you covered.

The chapters in this part show you how to set up shop with fixed wireless at home or in a small office. When you need to synch up data from your desktop to your PDA and take it with you, we'll show you the best wireless options. And so you keep your information safe, we'll run down some security measures that will let you get some sleep at night.

Safe and Secure in the Wireless Blue Yonder

In This Chapter

- ◆ Avoiding viruses and other Internet hazards
- ◆ Keeping your wireless equipment safe from dust, water, and thieves
- ◆ Breaking this is hard to do: ruggedized computers

Sure, I have some advice for you on wireless devices and how to use them. But that won't do you much good if somebody walks off with your PDA or starts snooping around on a computer on your wireless office network. At this point in the book, some security tips are in order.

While protecting your data and equipment is relatively straightforward with traditional desktop computers, the nature of wireless devices makes them more susceptible to hackers and theft.

Here are some things to consider:

◆ On the road, you can protect your two-way pager, smart phone, or other wireless device with inexpensive add-ons.

◆ If your equipment is swiped, you want to make sure the information on it is difficult to read.

◆ If you use wireless local area networking products (to connect the computers in your home or office), you can protect your network from hackers, so they won't use your computers for sending e-mail, hacking Web sites, and generally snooping around your stuff.

Safe Computing at Home

How can you protect your wireless home or office network? You'll likely want to learn a bit about firewalls and *encryption* (encoding your data). You might also need some outside assistance if your data is highly sensitive.

Well-Connected Words

Encryption converts data into a scrambled code so that it cannot (easily) be intercepted. Only those with authorization can read encrypted data.

Whether you're a single user at home surfing the Web or a business with sensitive data, you should check out Chapter 14, "Maintaining Wireless Networks," for more information on keeping your network secure.

Using a Firewall

A firewall is software, or a combination software and hardware device, that hides your computer or network when it's made available on the Internet. "Always-on" connections such as cable, DSL, and satellite Internet are more vulnerable to hackers, because they are connected full-time. As soon as you turn on your computer, you're up and running, and you're that much more open to malicious activity. ZoneAlarm (www.zonealarm.com) is an excellent program you can download and use for free for personal use. Business use costs $39.95 a year.

You can also buy a hardware firewall. If you have a router—a device for linking one network to another (for instance, your home or office computers to the Internet)—you might find that it includes an installed hardware firewall. Linux operating systems, such as Red Hat, come with a software firewall preinstalled.

Learning About PDA Viruses

When people talk about PDA viruses, they're primarily concerned with malicious programs that infect an office network when they're synched up at a desktop PC. Infected files from the PDA can be transferred to your desktop computer during data synchronization, which can infect others computers on a network.

There have not (yet) been reports of major damage due to PDA viruses. But any device that can open e-mail attachments, in particular, can be at risk. That includes smart phones with e-mail capability that can forward messages that have a virus attached.

As with desktop computers, the main risk is opening documents and e-mail attachments that contain a virus that could erase data from your local PC or network computers. Make sure you have antivirus software that scans your attachments before you open them. Some viruses replicate themselves once they've been opened and send themselves to everyone in your address book, which might cause your friends and co-workers to let their guard down. Never open an attachment from someone you don't know, and be wary of all attachments, even those from people you do know.

Virus Protection

You can protect your PDA from acquiring a virus in a handful of ways. And although most computer experts don't consider PDA viruses a major threat yet, the damage done is expected to increase greatly as more handhelds are enabled with wireless access.

Back up your handheld often, so you can do a "hard reset" (erasing all data on the handheld), then synch up with your desktop to put all your clean data back on your PDA.

Virus Fixes

In addition to simply using good common sense when opening attachments and synching up, you might also choose to install virus-scanning software on your home or office network.

If you do install antivirus software, make sure you use up-to-date definition files, which identify viruses that are currently infecting users' computers. You can usually download these for free, at software maker's Web sites. Most antivirus software reminds you to update your definition files every two weeks or so.

Antivirus software makers, including McAfee (www.mcafee.com) and Symantec (www.symantec.com), sell software you can install on your network to protect data from infected PDAs. The software typically runs between $25 to $40.

Secure Computing

Your desktop computer is unlikely to be swiped by a street thug or kicked by a wild animal. Sadly, if you travel often, the same can't be said for your wireless smart phone, laptop, or PDA.

Your equipment is more at risk if it's mobile. And, unfortunately, almost every type of wireless device is relatively easy to steal, whether it's mobile or fixed.

Synch Up

Are you nervous about losing your laptop? The Laptop Labeler is a $25 shareware program you can download that adds your name and phone number to a computer's boot sequence, which displays before the operating system starts. It can't be removed by reformatting the disk, and it can identify you as the rightful owner, every time the computer starts. You can download the Labeler at www.fringeweb.com/laplabl.html.

Ruggedized Computers

When we talk about wireless ruggedized computers, we're talking about machines that can take a beating (or a dunking). These machines cost a pretty penny, but if you're a mobile worker in a rough environment, they can be real lifesavers (see Figure 11.1). Plus, and this is important, they look really, really cool.

Figure 11.1

The Panasonic Toughbook is ready for a drop kick.

(Photo courtesy of Panasonic)

Ruggedized notebooks usually have several of the following:

◆ A shock-absorbing case that can take a fall of about three feet, with a similarly hearty hard drive that is gel-mounted to bounce back from a dropkicking.

◆ A case that keeps dust and liquids from entering the notebook.

◆ A water-resistant case and keyboard.

◆ A hard-shell for transporting the device without damaging it. (Note: Don't ever check your laptop when you fly.)

Panasonic's Toughbook (www.panasonic.com/toughbook) is a notable ruggedized notebook with wireless capabilities. Some come with built-in support for connecting to a wireless network (or another Toughbook) and wireless modems for connecting to the Internet.

Most ruggedized portables cost one and a half to two times as much as non-ruggedized computers. That's probably why you don't see too many of them on the subway. Ruggedized equipment is primarily used by the military, police, and fire and rescue workers.

Bet You Didn't Know

According to computer insurance agency Safeware (www.safeware. com), 25,000 computers were written off as a loss in 2000 due to water damage alone. Broken and damaged screens are some of the other common reasons computers are lost. Accidental damage is the number-one reason computers are written off (793,000 in 2000), with theft coming in second, at 387,000.

Water-Proofing

Can't afford a ruggedized notebook? No problem. You can take care of your own portable wireless equipment by purchasing cases that keep it safe.

For your cell phone or PDA, you can buy water-resistant cases to keep your equipment dry and offer a bit of padding, including neoprene (wet-suit material). Online vendors Road Warrior (www.roadwarrior.com) and iGo (www.igo.com) sell a number of inexpensive water-resistant cases for mobile phones, handhelds, and laptops.

Need something more substantial? Cell Safe (www.cellsafe.com) offers a number of hard-shell plastic cases for all types of mobile computers, including GPS (global positioning system) devices, for $25 to $30.

Theft

The thrill of mobile computing is coupled with the dangers of showing off your expensive electronics on the street. But fear not, all kinds of antitheft devices are available to help you protect your wireless goods (see Figure 11.2).

Figure 11.2

The alarming Targus Defcon laptop security device.

(Photo courtesy of Targus)

Locks, cords, and wires are still the theft-deterrents of choice, because of their simplicity and cost.

Keep in mind that your Pocket PC, Palm OS handheld, and likely your Web phone already come with preloaded password protection. If you're concerned about sensitive data on your handheld, be sure to use it.

Here's how to password protect a Pocket PC:

1. Select **Settings, Personal** tab, then **Password**.
2. Type a password, and select Require password when device is turned on.

Here's how to password protect a Palm OS handheld:

1. Select **Security** from the Applications menu (see Figure 11.3).

Figure 11.3

Select the Security application so that you can assign your handheld a password.

2. Click **Unassigned** (see Figure 11.4).

Figure 11.4

Click the Unassigned area, and you'll be prompted to enter a password.

3. Enter a password and click **OK** (see Figure 11.5).

Figure 11.5

Type in a password of your choice, and you can start sleeping again.

4. Click **Lock & Turn Off Device,** if you want to test your password.

Check out the following effective antitheft features for wireless devices:

♦ Kensington's MicroSaver is a theft deterrent that fits into the stylus holder of your PDA and secures your device to a stationary object (such as a desk). The device costs between $25 to $40. Kensington also makes a line of cables and locks for laptops and peripherals (www.kensington. com).

♦ The Targus Defcon is the disquieting name of, aptly, a sonic alarm for laptops. The battery-operated device has a motion sensor that goes off if the motion sensor is triggered or the cable connecting it to your laptop is cut. It runs about $50 (www.port.com).

♦ The bluVenom alarm (about $89) fits into the floppy drive of your computer and lets out a scream if the machine is moved too quickly (www.bluvenom.com).

♦ You can also find alarms that squeal when the unit gets to far away from you (www.trackitcorp.com) and even software that automatically tells you where your computer is once a perpetrator makes a connection to the Internet (www.computrace.com).

> **Watch Out!**
>
> Password protection can be a great way to keep your data safe. But what if you forget your password? You'll probably need to do a hard reset of your device, which erases all its data, and then synchronize your PDA and computer (to get all your data back) by placing the PDA in its cradle.

The Least You Need to Know

♦ Wireless devices, both stationary and portable, have more associated safety and security concerns than traditional, wired computing equipment.

♦ The combination of firewall and antivirus software is a good start in protecting your wireless local area network.

◆ If your wireless mobile needs protection from large amounts of dust or vibration, you can purchase heavy-duty wireless computers or waterproof cases to keep your equipment up and running.

◆ Wireless devices, often mobile, offer an appealing target for thieves. Any of a number of inexpensive antitheft devices can make your handheld and notebook computers safer.

Wireless Broadband

In This Chapter

- ◆ Setting up one-way satellite Internet access
- ◆ Two-way satellite technology
- ◆ Fast phones and modems
- ◆ Checking out fixed wireless

Tired of waiting for pages to download when you're surfing? Long file downloads got you down? There's a lot of talk these days about using the Internet, wirelessly, at very high speed.

It's no wonder when you consider that most people can't surf wirelessly faster than 14.4kbps. You've probably heard about cable and DSL modems, which are fast Internet services provided by the phone or cable company. After you've played around with a speedy, dedicated Internet connection at work, such as a T-1 line, or a cable or DSL modem, it's hard to go back to slow surfing.

Given the rise in cellular phone use, and the projections that more people will surf the Web wirelessly than will use wired connections, it's just a matter of time before you're surfing speedily, from wherever you are.

In addition, fast satellite Internet access is ready right now. If you live in an area that doesn't get DSL or cable access, satellite can be the only way to get high-speed Internet access.

Fast Phones: 3G Speed on the Go

Smart phones are great for picking up e-mail, but using them to browse the Internet can be a chore because of their pokiness.

Wireless phone carriers are working on a high-speed cellular phone technology called 3G (third generation) that should speed things up.

At expected data transfer speeds of between 64kbps to 384kbps (depending on how fast you're moving), 3G technology promises more multimedia capabilities on your phone, such as the ability to download music and watch videos.

In the meantime, wireless phone providers are working on rolling out what is called 2.5G, a stopgap between 2G (current digital) phones and the speedy 3G phones of the future.

GPRS (General Packet Radio Service)

One of the more promising, currently available mobile phone technologies is General Packet Radio Service, also called GPRS. AT&T Wireless Group is testing this high-speed service, which offers a maximum speed of 144kbps. GPRS is considered a 2.5G technology.

Motorola's Timeport 7382i is the first wireless phone that can make use of the high-speed service in North America. Unfortunately, the phone can support speeds of only 30kbps to 40kbps. The service has been tested in Seattle, and faster phones are expected soon.

Service is usually charged by the amount of information transferred, rather than air minutes, as with most cell phones. For $50, you get 1MB of data and 400 voice minutes.

Nokia is also planning on releasing GPRS phones in the United States, and phone service for GPRS is expected from AT&T Wireless, Cingular, and VoiceStream.

One-Way Satellite: Speed at Home

If you need fast Internet access, are on a budget, and can't get cable or DSL access (because of your location), Hughes Network's DirecPC service might appeal to you.

DirecPC one-way satellite service is sometimes called a telco-return connection, because you use a satellite link to download data and a telephone line to upload data. What's that mean to you? Well, you'll download faster than you upload. In most cases that's no big problem because whatever you want to download (a Web page, a photo, or a program) is usually quite a bit larger than what you're uploading (the request for information that is sent when you click a link on the Web).

DirecPC could be the way to go, if you don't plan to do a lot of large file uploads. Large uploads might include sending e-mail attachments or, while working on your own Web page, copying documents to a Web server for other folks on the Web to see.

The main drawback with one-way DirecPC service is that when you surf the Web or check e-mail, you'll be tying up a phone line. And your upload speed is determined by the speed of your (most likely 56kbps) modem. Special software that you install on your computer sends data through your phone line to your Internet service provider (you can use DirecPC as your ISP or another of your choice). The data is sent to DirecPC's operations center, to the Web server that has the page you want to see, and beamed 22,300 miles up to the satellite, then back down to your PC.

Some one-way satellite pros:

- Faster than analog modems (400kbps download). Upload speed depends on your modem (likely slightly less than 56kbps).
- Reasonable price.

Some one-way satellite cons:

- No competition. The sole one-way satellite provider is DirecPC, from Hughes Network Systems.
- One-way satellite ties up a phone line.

Well-Connected Words

Latency is the noticeable delay in the time between when you click a link while surfing the Web on your computer and when you receive a Web page, by way of a satellite 22,300 miles above.

◆ *Latency* (the delay between when you click a link and when the data arrives).

You'll pay about $40 a month for unlimited access. That's quite a bargain, though you need to pony up another $10 a month if you want DirecPC to act as your ISP. The equipment costs around $400, with professional installation (not a bad idea) costing around $200.

Two-Way Satellite

The introduction of two-way satellite (also called Satellite Return System, or simply SRS) addresses two big problems with the previous generation of satellite Internet access:

◆ Two-way satellite doesn't tie up a phone line.

◆ Download *and* upload speeds are faster (about 400 to 500kbps when downloading and 128 to 153kbps when uploading).

Two-way service beams your request for a Web page from your antenna, not through your phone, so latency is less of a problem (but 22,300 miles is still a long way to go to ask for a Web page).

There are two main providers of two-way satellite Internet access:

◆ **DirecWay (www.direcway.com).** Like DirecPC, this is a service of Hughes Network Systems, which also sells the DirecTV (satellite TV programming) services. Expect to pay about $400 for the satellite dish, satellite modem, and receiver and about $200 for professional installation of the dish. Monthly service runs about $69.95 for unlimited access. DirecWay doesn't sell the dishes or service directly. You can find a provider at the company's Web site, or call your local satellite TV service provider, using the old-fashioned Yellow Pages. And, importantly, you might be able to find promotions for free installation through some providers.

◆ **StarBand (www.starband.com).** As with DirecWay, distributors set the pricing for this two-way satellite service (see Figure 12.1). Pricing might run as high as $400 for equipment, but keep an eye out for discounts and other deals on the Web. Installation and monthly service run about the same price as for DirecWay ($200/$70 month, respectively).

Figure 12.1

A StarBand Model 360 satellite modem.

(Photo courtesy of StarBand Communications, Inc.)

Unlike cable and DSL, satellite service can be affected by weather. Providers say cloudy days and light rain don't interfere with service, though a heavy downpour can reduce performance and could even knock out service while you wait for a storm to pass.

Neither provider supports satellite Internet access on the Macintosh. You can, however, use two-way satellite service on a Macintosh if you first set up a network with a PC-based proxy server (see Figure 12.2). Setting up a Mac to work with StarBand is (well) beyond the scope of this chapter. Christopher Breen wrote an excellent article, called "Broadband in the Boonies, Part II," for *Macworld* magazine, on painfully setting up his Mac to use StarBand. You can search for the article at www.macworld.com.

Figure 12.2

With two-way satellite Internet access, your antenna sends and receives data to a satellite 22,300 miles above the earth.

(Photo courtesy of StarBand Communications, Inc.)

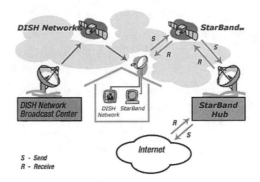

Both the two-way satellite providers require that a professional install the dish. Reasonably handy people could install one-way satellite on their own. But because two-way satellite uploads data to a satellite, the positioning process is much more difficult than setting up a one-way dish.

- ◆ **Product:** DirecPC, one-way satellite Internet service, www.direcpc.com

  Price: $400 for equipment, $200 average installation, $40 to $50 monthly fee

  Speed: 400kpbs download, analog phone 56kpbs upload

  Requirements: 200Mhz Pentium PC, 32MB RAM, 20 to 120MB free hard drive space, free USB or PCI port, Windows 98 or higher

  Where to buy: Local vendors and electronics retailers (Circuit City, Best Buy, etc.)

- ◆ **Product:** DirecWay, two-way satellite Internet service, www. direcway.com

  Price: Varies (widely) by vendor, but averages about $500 for equipment, with $200 for installation, and $69.99 for monthly service; keep an eye out for deals, including price breaks for bundling with ISP service (see providers in Where to buy)

  Speed: 400kpbs download, 128kpbs upload

  Requirements: Pentium II PC, 333Mhz, 32MB RAM, 20 to 120MB free hard drive space, free USB port, Windows 98 or greater

  Where to buy: Online, through authorized distributors including Earthlink, AOL Plus, and Pegasus which also supply the monthly service

◆ **Product:** StarBand, two-way satellite service, www.starband.com

Price: $500 for equipment, $200 average installation, $69.99 monthly fee

Speed: 500kpbs download, 150kbps upload

Requirements: Pentium II, 333Mhz, 64MB RAM, 120MB free hard drive space, free USB port or Ethernet Windows 98 or greater

Where to buy: Online, authorized distributors including Dish Network and Primus Telecommunications

Watch Out!

You can purchase a StarBand satellite and service at some Radio Shack stores (not all sell the satellite and service, so call ahead), but you must also purchase a Compaq computer to go with it, not such a hot deal if you want to use your computer to go online with satellite Internet access. Check the StarBand Web site's "Where to Buy" section for information on finding a reseller who can sell you the service for the computer you already own.

Stationary Broadband

Like satellite, fixed wireless, a stationary broadband technology, is an especially attractive offering in places that cable or DSL broadband service isn't available. Fixed wireless is aimed at home and office use.

Watch Out!

If you are interested in wireless broadband Internet access for your home or office, currently, you are much more likely to be able to get satellite Internet access than fixed wireless. Note also that some providers, such as WorldCom, concentrate on business customers. You can check availability at Sprint (www.sprintbroadband.com), WorldCom (www.worldcom.com/us/products/access/broadband/wireless/), and AT&T (www.iatt.com).

Here's how it works. A radio transmitter/receiver installed at your location, sometimes an antenna attached to the outside or your house, picks up signals from your service provider's wireless base station. Service varies widely, by provider, which might be a small, mom-and-pop operation or a large phone company (Sprint, AT&T, and WorldCom are among those offering limited fixed wireless Internet access). Speeds can reach those of fast digital lines, such as a T1 (1.5 megabits per second).

The real benefit of fixed wireless, however, is how fast you can get started. You don't have to wait for a technician to come in and install a line. I recently ordered digital subscriber line (DSL) service for a small business, and the wait time from the local phone company was 50 days—at best. Some small ISPs set up their fixed wireless customers in less than a week.

Fixed wireless is a way to access the Internet using radio waves. Your computer makes a request using a broadband modem, which is connected to an external transceiver, mounted outside your home or office (see Figure 12.3). The request is sent to a radio transmission tower and routed to the Internet.

Figure 12.3

Need speed? Try fixed wireless, if it's available in your area.

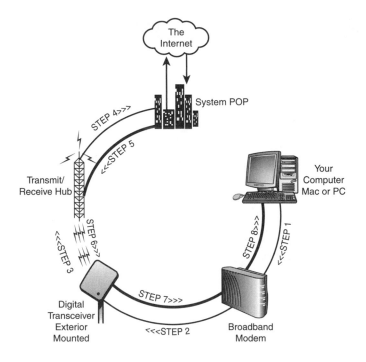

The Least You Need to Know

◆ Fast phones, which will enable you to access the Web at speeds approaching those of home broadband, are on the way. 3G will also bring us a variety of mobile nonphone devices such as picture phones and multimedia players.

◆ One-way satellite is an inexpensive option for folks without cable or DSL access. The downside: The service, called DirecWay, ties up a phone line.

◆ Two-way satellite offers fast downloading (as when you view a Web page) and uploading (such as when you send an e-mail attachment). Two-way satellite service keeps your phone line free and is available, like one-way satellite, anywhere you can get a clear view of the sky.

◆ Fixed wireless is a broadband wireless service that's gaining popularity, primarily in cities, where DSL and cable service isn't available. Fixed wireless service can be set up quickly but is less widely available than satellite Internet access.

Chapter 3

Starting a Wireless Network

In This Chapter

- ◆ Where to put your network devices
- ◆ Installing your wireless network cards
- ◆ Installing your software
- ◆ Enabling encryption

You've got computers. The Internet has tons of cool stuff. Why not get them together?

Well, you probably have plenty of good reasons for not yet starting a network. First, networking sounds complicated. But it's not. Wireless networking dramatically decreases the time it takes to get all your computers online.

In this chapter, we'll use 802.11b wireless networking, the fastest standard currently available and connect several desktop or laptop computers together. They'll all be able to share files and an Internet connection.

Although this seems like an incredibly geeky way to spend an afternoon, it's … well, frankly, a pretty geeky way to spend an afternoon. But networking your computers will make them dramatically easier to use. You won't have to copy files from one computer to another using floppy disks. And networking means you can stop fighting for Internet access on the one connected machine in your house: Now all your machines can get online via the network.

Starting a Home Network

For this example, we'll set up a network of three computers, using equipment you can find at any electronics and office supply stores.

You will typically have a choice of three types of wireless adapter cards for your computers. Here are a few examples of how you might network your computers:

- A laptop or PDA, connected to the network with a wireless network card adapter that fits into the PC Card slot of a laptop
- A desktop computer, connected to the network with an internal PCI wireless networking card
- A desktop PC, connected to the network with a USB wireless network adapter

One good point about wireless networking is the ability to mix and match hardware made by different manufacturers. If all the manufacturers use the same standard, such as 802.11b (a.k.a. Wi-Fi), they should all work together.

The installation and configuration of wireless network cards vary by manufacturer. Make sure you read the instructions for your equipment. Important: Your manufacturer might require that you follow these steps in a different order.

Peer-to-Peer or Infrastructure?

First things first. You must decide how your networked devices will communicate. Wireless networks are usually set up in one of two ways:

♦ *Ad hoc* **(also known as peer-to-peer).** In this setup, each computer you want to put on the network needs a wireless networking card. The computers connect directly to each other.

♦ *Infrastructure.* In this configuration, all your wireless access cards communicate with the access point. The access point can be connected to your existing network if you have one. It can also be used to connect to a *router*, which can be used to share a cable or DSL modem on your network (more on routers in Chapter 14, "Maintaining Wireless Networks").

An ad hoc network is inexpensive to set up and a good bet if you simply want to share files between computers. An access point also extends the range of your wireless network (see Figure 13.1). If you want to connect your wirelessly networked computers to the Internet, you can purchase an access point and connect it to a router (some access points include built-in routers for this purpose).

Well-Connected Words

In an **ad hoc** wireless network configuration, each computer you want to connect to the network needs a wireless networking card. The computers will connect directly to each other. In an **infrastructure** network, by contrast, wireless network cards all communicate with a central *access point*. A **router** enables you to connect two networks. You can use a router to give multiple computers the capability to share a single Internet connection. For example, to set up your computers to share a DSL modem, you can plug a router into one port in a hub, plug a modem in another port, and plug your computers in the rest of the available ports. You'll be surfing in no time.

Wireless network cards installed in a PC and laptop connect to a wireless access point (see Figure 13.2). The access point connects to a router, which, connected to a cable or DSL modem, provides the network access to the Internet.

Figure 13.1

An access point connects a wireless network to a wired network and helps extend the range of your network.

(Photo courtesy of Xircom, Inc.)

Figure 13.2

A sample wireless network.

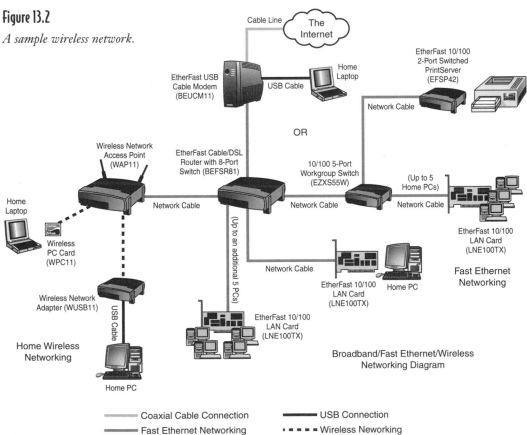

Cable Line

The Internet

EtherFast USB Cable Modem (BEUCM11)

USB Cable

Home Laptop

EtherFast 10/100 2-Port Switched PrintServer (EFSP42)

Network Cable

OR

Wireless Network Access Point (WAP11)

EtherFast Cable/DSL Router with 8-Port Switch (BEFSR81)

10/100 5-Port Workgroup Switch (EZXS55W)

(Up to 5 Home PCs)

Home Laptop

Network Cable

Network Cable

Network Cable

Wireless PC Card (WPC11)

(Up to an additional 5 PCs)

EtherFast 10/100 LAN Card (LNE100TX)

Wireless Network Adapter (WUSB11)

USB Cable

Network Cable

EtherFast 10/100 LAN Card (LNE100TX)

Home PC

Fast Ethernet Networking

Home Wireless Networking

EtherFast 10/100 LAN Card (LNE100TX)

Broadband/Fast Ethernet/Wireless Networking Diagram

Home PC

Coaxial Cable Connection

USB Connection

Fast Ethernet Networking

Wireless Neworking

Installing Your Card

Now that you know the layout (a.k.a. *topography*) of your network, you need to connect adapter cards to each of your computers. No worries, my soon-to-be wireless friend. This is the easy part.

1. Turn off your computer and unplug it. (Some people leave their computer plugged in while installing network cards, and some unplug. I fit comfortably into the unplug camp.)

2. Connect your wireless network adapter to your computer (see Figure 13.3).

   If your desktop computers have USB connections, you might choose an adapter that can plug into this speedy port. The maximum data rate of USB, 12mbps, is a good match for the maximum bandwidth of an 802.11b wireless network at 11mpbs. The main benefit of USB is an easy installation. You don't have to open your computer to install the card. Just plug into the USB port and you're off and running.

   Laptops are also quite easy to bring onto the network. Just purchase a PC Card wireless network adapter, and insert it into the PC Card slot of your laptop.

   Connecting a desktop with a PCI adapter is the trickiest installation because it often requires two pieces of equipment: the PCI card and a wireless network adapter. To install the PCI adapter, open the case of your computer. Unscrew the metal cover near the back of the computer. Insert the PCI card into an open PCI slot on the computer, and fasten the screw to keep it in place. In many cases, you will need to then insert a wireless PC Card network adapter into the slot in the PCI card you install. This setup takes quite a bit more time, and if often more expensive, than installing a wireless USB network adapter.

Figure 13.3

A wireless PC Card adapter.

(Photo courtesy of Buffalo Technology, Inc.)

3. After installing your wireless network adapter, you need to restart your computer. In the next section, we'll go over basic software configuration. Once again, keep in mind that some manufacturers will have you do these steps in a different order—follow the steps that come with your equipment.

During installation, just in case, keep a copy of your operating system nearby. You might be prompted to insert it into your CD-ROM drive so that your computer can copy files from your OS disk to your computer before you can finish booting up.

Installing Software

The software that comes bundled with your wireless networking equipment should automatically install the driver that enables your computer to communicate with the network card (see Figure 13.4). Then the software steps you through a series of configuration selections.

Figure 13.4

Installing the software for a wireless USB network card.

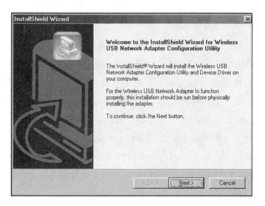

You'll probably need to select either ad hoc or infrastructure mode on a menu during the installation process (see Figure 13.5).

The software that comes with your wireless network adapter will likely tell you when you have a connection to another card or your access point and might express the degree of signal strength.

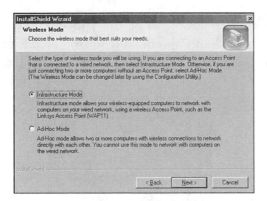

Figure 13.5

Choosing ad hoc or infra-structure mode. In ad hoc mode, computers communicate directly with each other. In infrastructure mode, the computers communicate through a wireless device called an access point.

As your adapters are placed further from each other, the speed of data transmission is lessened. Data speed drops, as you get farther away, in this order:

◆ 11mbps

◆ 5.5mbps

◆ 2mbps

◆ 1mbps

Many adapters automatically set the data rate based on the strength of the signal. You might also be able to set it manually, which is helpful if you notice that the rate varies quite a bit. You can then set it to a rate that it will consistently maintain.

Enabling Encryption

Now you need to decide whether to enable encryption. Encryption encodes your data so hackers can't intercept your data as it travels through the air. The tradeoff is that encryption slows down the speed of transmission, and therefore slows down your network.

"Enable encryption," you might say, "Who, me?" Sounds tricky, right? Don't worry, most wireless networking equipment comes with a straightforward set of steps for turning on encryption. Encrypting your data can be as simple as clicking a button when prompted during installation.

Your network card will likely ask you *what level* of encryption you want. You can disable encryption, which is probably the default setting (see Figure 13.6). That might be fine for you, if you're not concerned about people letting themselves onto your network.

Figure 13.6

Enabling encryption on a wireless network card.

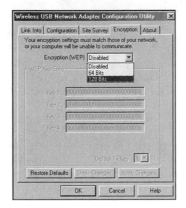

You'll likely see a lower level of encryption (such as 64-bit) and a higher level (such as 128-bit). Importantly, make sure that all your wireless devices (your network cards and wireless adapter, for instance) are using the same level of encryption, or they will not connect.

Okay, take a deep breath. Setting up a wireless network is supposed to be easy, right? Keep these thoughts in mind:

◆ If you read the instructions that came with your wireless network equipment, you can often get up and running without making any configuration changes. Most equipment starts communication using the default settings. In fact, messing around with the configuration utility too much is a pretty sure way to make sure your network *won't work*.

◆ Try the default settings first, right out of the box. If that doesn't work, make sure all the settings on each computer are the same.

◆ Often, when first installing your wireless network, it's helpful to start with encryption turned off. After you get your computers connected over the network, go back and turn on encryption.

◆ If you're stumped then, try the vendor's Web site for more information, and if that doesn't work, it's time to call tech support.

Adding an Access Point

Earlier in the chapter you found out that adding a piece of equipment called an access point is a good way to tie wired and wireless networks together. An access point acts as a wireless hub and extends the range of your wireless network, essentially doubling the range of two computers communicating with wireless network cards.

If you have more than one access point, you can *roam*, or maintain your connection as you move around your home and office, passing from the coverage area of one access point to another.

When you place your access point carefully, you open up more area for transmitting data on your wireless network. Try to find a place for your access point that puts it near the center of your wireless network cards. You get more range from an access point that is in a high position with as few obstructions as possible. You might even see some speed improvement by adjusting the angle of your antennas.

You can plug an access point into an Ethernet hub, or connect it directly to a router for sharing a single Internet connection, such as a cable or DSL modem.

You can also add wireless networking to your PDA. Several manufactures sell CompactFlash or PC Card adapters that let handhelds get in on the wireless network action.

The Least You Need to Know

◆ You can add wireless capability to your computer using a PC Card adapter (primarily for laptops or handhelds) or USB adapter. You can also open your computer and insert a PCI add-in card into a free slot.

◆ You can set up your network in an ad hoc mode, in which your wireless network cards communicate directly with each other. You can also set up your network in an infrastructure mode, where your network cards communicated directly with a device called an access point.

◆ An access point (AP) can help you extend the range of your network and tie your wireless network into a wired Ethernet network.

◆ Routers can be used to connect networks to each other. In most cases, you would add a router to your network to enable multiple computers to share a single Internet connection.

◆ If you are concerned about the security of your network, you should enable encryption using the software that comes with your wireless networking equipment.

Maintaining Wireless Networks

In This Chapter

◆ Adding equipment to your wireless network

◆ More on hubs and routers

◆ Network security concerns

◆ Having fun with wireless networks

Okay, so now what? This is the question people all over the world are asking themselves as they finish connecting their wireless networks.

Setting up a wireless network is simple, and keeping it running is uncomplicated. After you have everything up and running, a wireless network pretty much takes care of itself.

As the number of computers in your home or office grows, you might want to add new equipment. If you give a little thought to your network before setting it up, you can add relatively inexpensive Ethernet (wired) hubs and routers to expand it. We'll consider what to look for as you shop for hardware to expand your existing network.

You might want to increase the level of security on your network as you begin to learn more about it. There are inexpensive and easy-to-install ways to keep your network secure.

And networks don't have to be so boring. Half the point of having a network is getting some fun out of it. You can play network games, listen to music from one computer on another, and surf the Web while you sit on your porch. In this chapter, we'll also look at the lighter side of wireless networking.

Adding Equipment

If you happen to be scanning the Sunday newspaper ads and see a great deal on a wireless network adapter, you're in luck. Most adapters that use the 802.11b standard are interoperable. You can buy a card from one manufacturer and be pretty sure it works with a card from another. Your wireless access point (which connects your wireless network to wired devices, such as a cable modem) can be from Orinoco, and your wireless network adapter can be from NetGear, D-Link, Linksys, 3Com, or other 802.11b network card manufacturer.

An example of a Linksys wireless access point and router is in Figure 14.1. Plug the Ethernet cable from your DSL or cable modem into the WAN port. Then connect your computers using wireless network cards installed in each machine. The four Ethernet ports on the back of the access point can be used to connect computers by Ethernet cables. The uplink port can be used to connect the access point to other hubs or switches on the network.

Figure 14.1

A Linksys wireless access point and router.

Make sure that the card is interoperable. Cards displaying the Wi-Fi logo are certified to work together. And most cards that say (right on the box, or their Web site) that they support the 802.11b standard should work together. You can see a listing of cards that are certified to interoperate at this Web site: www.wi-fi.com/certified_products.asp.

That said, some cards are specifically made to handle certain duties, such as carrying multimedia for music and video. These cards might use a standard that does not work with other wireless networking cards. Check to make sure you know what you're getting.

The networking equipment maker NetGear offers a good example. One Netgear wireless networking card is specifically sold to be used for multimedia; another, which uses the 802.11b standard, can be mixed with other 802.11b equipment. If multimedia is your prime concern, you can purchase a network card optimized for multimedia, but it might be at the expense of interoperability with other 802.11b cards.

Keep in mind that you can buy, and use together, more equipment than just wireless adapter cards. You can mix and match 802.11b access points, PC Cards, USB adapter cards, PCI cards, and printer servers.

A (wireless or wired) printer server is a device that enables you to add a printer onto a network without first connecting it to a computer (see Figure 14.2). The print server can help speed up your computing, because it uses its memory to handle the printing rather than that of the computer from which you're printing. The freed up memory on your computer can be used for more useful activities—like a network game.

Figure 14.2

All access pass: a Buffalo Technology wireless printer server, the AirStation.

(Photo courtesy of Buffalo Technology, Inc.)

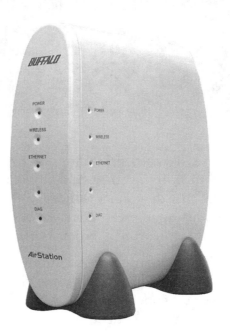

Synch Up

A handful of network providers can help you connect a quick, wireless connection to the Internet when you travel. Wayport (www.wayport.com) is often found in hotels and airports. Need a hot cup of java or a massage? Check out MobileStar (www.mobilestar.com), which provides network access at Starbucks, hotels and resorts, restaurants, and airport lounges nationwide. AirWave (www.airwave.com) provides free network access in the San Francisco Bay area (right across the street from my old office, actually … sigh … I left my network connection in San Francisco).

More on Hubs and Routers

What would you say if your neighbor asks you to help him set up a wireless network? My advice: It depends on how much you like your neighbor, and if he returns the lawnmower on time.

If you agree to help, then you can let him onto your network when he comes over for coffee. In the meantime, you might want to think about hubs and routers.

To share an Internet connection, you'll likely need a router and you might need a hub or *switch*, if you have—or want to add—computers wired with Ethernet to your network.

So what should you look for in a hub? Check out the following:

> **Synch Up**
>
> A hub enables you to plug in several devices using Ethernet ports. Each of the devices connected to the hub can then communicate with the others. For instance, you could plug your wired cable modem, a wireless access point, and a computer into your hub. Each has access to what you put on the network, whether it's wired or not.

- If your hub is wireless, again, *interoperability is important.* If you're using the 802.11b wireless standard, you want to make sure the hub can work with other 802.11b equipment, like network cards and access points.

- Should you buy a hub or a switch? In most cases, a hub works fine and costs quite a bit less than a switch. A hub lets each computer access the others on the network, but a switch can let many computers access files at the same time. A *switch* intelligently handles data (see Figure 14.3), looking for the best possible route to your computer and increasing throughput; a hub just repeats the data through all the ports in the hub.

> **Well-Connected Words**
>
> A **switch** connects computers together in a traditional, wired Ethernet network. A switch can also be used to create a subnetwork, so that the computers plugged into it don't affect the larger network traffic. You can connect a switch as a standalone element of your network, or your access point might have a switch built in.

Figure 14.3

A switch will let you connect multiple computers by Ethernet cable and transfer data between them at higher throughput than a hub.

(*Photo courtesy of NETGEAR*)

To connect a hub, all you need to do is plug one end of a cable (usually Ethernet or USB) into your network card on your computer and plug the other end into the hub. The hub shares the data sent from each computer, so all the other computers plugged into the hub have access to it.

Routers are another important way to share multiple networks. In our neighbor's case, he could plug in a router that makes it possible for his cable modem connection to be shared by all computers in his house. A router could also be used to share Windows, Mac, and Linux computers that all speak different languages on their own networks.

If you look for a wireless access point to add to your wireless network, you might consider one that (for just a little more money) includes a router. You can then both connect all your computers for sharing files between them and connect them all to the Internet.

Alternatively, you can use a wired router and hub to get your computers on the Internet. Later, you can add a wireless access point and plug it into the hub. You can then share wired computers (plugged into the hub by Ethernet) and computers connected to the network using wireless network cards.

Synch Up

If your computer is connected to a wireless network, you can share any printers on the network. You can also share CD-ROMs, files on hard drives, and removable media, such as Iomega Zip disk drives.

When you shop for a router, make sure it includes a firewall to hide your network from hackers—no small matter. That shouldn't be a problem because routers typically have security features built in, such as a firewall and the ability to block users from accessing certain aspects of the Web, such as newsgroups or Web sites. You might want this kind of control if your company has a strict Internet use policy.

If you have just one computer on the Internet, you might consider installing firewall software, like the excellent ZoneAlarm (www.zonelabs.com), which is free for personal use. Note, however, that personal firewall software can disrupt your access to a network.

About Security

In Chapter 13, "Starting a Wireless Network," we talked a bit about security. Because security and privacy are important concerns, we elaborate on the topic a bit here.

Generally speaking, you want more than one layer of defense for your wireless network. If you ride a motorcycle, you wear a helmet and boots. If you connect a fast Internet connection, you lean on multiple safeguards.

First, you need to turn on encryption at every point in your network. If you use wireless network adapters only (in an ad hoc network, as described in Chapter 13), use the software that comes with your network cards to enable encryption. If you use an access point (in an infrastructure network), turn on encryption at the access point as well. The instructions that came with your equipment show you how.

Wireless networks use the *wireless equivalent privacy* (*WEP*), which enables you to scramble your data as it's transmitted between computers. You also need to choose a level of encryption. For instance, 128-bit encryption is more difficult to crack than 40-bit encryption.

Synch Up

Data is encrypted, or scrambled, using a mathematical formula called an algorithm. The algorithm is based on a key, a string of characters you need to provide, which could be a password. A 128-bit key is extremely hard to crack. Only the person who has the key should be able to decode the encrypted data.

Well-Connected Words

WEP (wireless equivalent privacy) is a method of encrypting data over a wireless 802.11b network. This protocol is meant to protect wireless LANs (local area networks), which are inherently more vulnerable to unauthorized access since the network data is transferred over radio waves.

If you're concerned about someone reading your e-mail and other data, encrypt it using pretty good privacy (PGP). This cryptography software converts data into code that you can transmit safely over a network. PGPmail and PGPfile are two programs you can use to encrypt files you e-mail or store on your network. You can find more about them at www.pgp.com. And you can download a free version of PGP (for Mac and PC, among other operating systems) from MIT's Web site at web.mit.edu/network/pgp.html.

There's nothing scary about setting up your network securely. However, you should make sure to …

◆ Follow the instructions that come with your wireless networking encryption for enabling encryption on your wireless network cards (and access point, if you have one).

◆ Use a firewall. A simple way to get firewall protection is to purchase a wireless access point that includes a router and firewall. When you plug in the access point to your network, your network will be hidden to hackers.

Multimedia over Your Network

I told you networks could be fun, but we haven't done a lot to prove it. Don't be scared off by all this security talk—being able to play games over a fast-running network, share Internet access, and watch videos from one PC on another is half the reason to link up.

Remember that neighbor, the one who wants to tap into your network, but won't return your garden weasel? You can take out your aggression by playing him in a network game. Check out all the network-friendly games at www.gamespot.com or www.download.com. Most games enable you to play against each other or play as a team. With a fast Internet connection, shared wirelessly, you can play against people all across the Internet from any computer in your house.

The really cool part of the whole thing is that most people have to use their computers near their network cables, but you're wire-free and can play from wherever you want!

Say you want to listen to a CD that's in a computer upstairs. Just share the CD player and you're set. If MP3 files are on the hard drive, you can click to launch them on the computer you're sharing and hear them through the speakers on your computer.

Although we've looked primarily at 802.11b networks, there are other wireless network technologies you should consider. And here's why.

The wireless network technology HomeRF is touted for its multimedia capabilities, despite its slower speed (1.6mpbs versus the 11mbps speed of 802.11b). That said, HomeRF has another benefit: You can use a HomeRF network to manage telephone calls as well as network your computers. (Note: Some companies that make wireless networking equipment are developing products that use the 802.11b standard for networking and are capable of wirelessly transmitting multimedia without degradation of picture or sound.)

There are lots of HomeRF products available, made by well-known manufacturers, including Intel and Proxim, and sometimes, importantly, at significantly less cost. Many users report good results with HomeRF networks, especially for listening to audio and video over the Internet (also known as *streaming*).

Well-Connected Words

Streaming allows you to watch or listen to multimedia as it downloads to your computer (instead of waiting for the entire file to download, and then viewing). Wireless networks are handy for using streaming multimedia, since you can check out audio and video from another computer on your network anywhere in your house. You can take your laptop out by the pool and watch a video on the hard drive of your PC upstairs.

If multimedia is your most important concern, look for wireless network equipment that supports the kinds of applications you plan to use. If you don't mind the lack of interoperability and slower file transfers, you're set. Many users laud HomeRF products for their ease of use and deft handling of multimedia.

The Least You Need to Know

- Wireless networks enable you to add new equipment, and if you choose carefully, you might be able to mix equipment from different manufacturers. You can add a new computer to the network by plugging in a new wireless network card.

- Hubs and routers are two ways to expand your network. You can save money by using a wired hub or router. You're still able to pick up your computer and take it with you.

- Use several levels of security to keep your network safe. Firewalls, wireless equivalent privacy (WEP), and pretty good privacy (PGP) can all be important parts of your security plan.

- You can use wireless networks to play games, listen to a CD playing on a computer in another room, and generally have a lot more fun on the Internet.

- Before you settle on a particular network standard, keep in mind that some network technologies are better at handling multimedia than others. This benefit might come at the cost of being able to buy equipment from different manufacturers and interoperability.

Home Network Walkthrough

In This Chapter

- ◆ Networking Windows 95/98/Me
- ◆ Installing protocols
- ◆ Identifying your computer
- ◆ Starting printer and file sharing
- ◆ Networking Windows 2000
- ◆ Troubleshooting

Over the last couple chapters you've read a lot about setting up equipment for a wireless network. If your hardware maker was thoughtful and provided you with networking software to get all your machines connected, you should be up and running.

If your hardware did not come with software to let you share files and printers on your network, we'll show you how to get Windows computers to start communicating. And you'll see how to share an Internet connection.

Here's our scenario:

♦ We have several computers running Windows 98 and Windows 2000 in the same home (it could also be a small office).

♦ Each computer has a wireless networking card.

♦ The wireless networking cards communicate with an access point, which includes a router (see Chapter 13, "Starting a Wireless Network," for more on this networking setup, called infrastructure mode).

♦ The router allows the network to connect to a cable or DSL modem. An access point with a built-in router is highly recommended, as it will make setting up your computers to communicate on the Internet much simpler. No router? That's okay. You can share an Internet connection using software that comes with Windows 98 Second Edition (SE) or higher. That gets slightly trickier, but it's certainly doable.

What Do You Need to Install?

Here's the basic overview. We'll install a protocol from your Windows OS disk called TCP/IP, which will let your computer communicate with your network and the Internet. If you're not using a router, we'll install another protocol, called NetBEUI, which comes with Windows. A protocol is a set of rules that define how communication takes place on your network.

Then we'll name your computer (something snappy) so that you can identify it on your network. We'll assign it to a workgroup. We'll set up printer sharing. And if you use Windows 2000, we'll set up user names and passwords for each person who will access your Windows 2000 computer. (Note that Windows 95/98/Me does not require this step.) Keep your OS disc handy, as well as the manufacturer's information on the type of card you have installed.

Installing TCP/IP for Windows 95/98/Me

A simple way to connect your computers to each other, and the Internet, is to use *TCP/IP*, the common communications standard for the Internet.

Most likely the software that came with your wireless networking adapter installed TCP/IP on your computer. If not, follow these steps:

1. To get started adding the TCP/IP protocol, we need first to open the Network dialog box. Double-click the **Network icon** in the Control Panel (see Figure 15.1). (To open the Control Panel, select **Start, Settings, Control Panel.**)

Well-Connected Words

TCP/IP (transmission control protocol/Internet protocol) is a protocol that allows computers to communicate over any network, whether at your home or office, or throughout the world in the form of the Internet. Every computer connected to the Internet, be it UNIX, Apple, PC, or any other, must speak TCP/IP. TCP/IP makes sure that all the bytes sent by one machine are received by the intended machine.

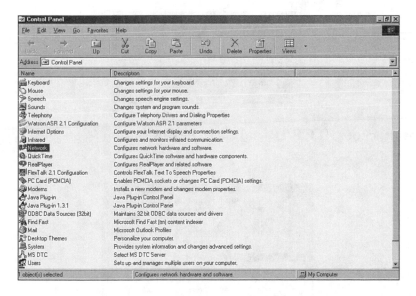

Figure 15.1

Open the Network dialog box.

2. Choose your wireless network card from the list, and click the **Add** button (see Figure 15.2). If you don't see your card, you might need to reinstall the software that came with it.

Figure 15.2

Choose your wireless network card.

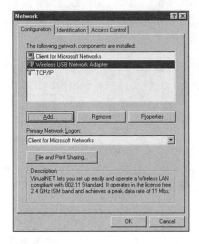

3. Select **Protocol** and click the **Add** button (see Figure 15.3).

Figure 15.3

Adding a network component.

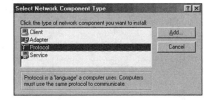

4. Select **Microsoft,** choose **TCP/IP,** and click the **OK** button (see Figure 15.4).

Figure 15.4

Adding TCP/IP.

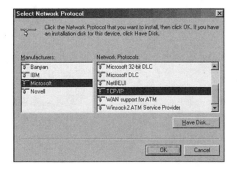

You might be prompted to insert your Windows operating system disk. If so, insert the disk in the drive and follow the screen prompts.

Note: If you do not have a router, you should also install NetBEUI (pronounced *net-boo-ey*), in addition to TCP/IP. Doing so will allow you to more easily share files and printers on your network. Choose **Add, Protocol, Microsoft, NetBEUI.** This protocol allows your computers to view each other and share resources on the network. If you have a router, you won't need to install it because TCP/IP will do the trick. All set? Let's give your computer a name if it hasn't got one already.

Synch Up

You can also open the Network dialog box by going to your Desktop and right-clicking **Network Neighborhood** (in Windows 95/98) or **Network Places** (in Windows 2000) and choosing **Properties.**

Identifying Your Computer

Now it's time to give your computer a name. Here we'll also assign your computer a *workgroup*, a group of machines on your network that will appear when you open Network Neighborhood from your desktop.

Each computer should have the same workgroup name (you can have more than one workgroup, but all the computers you want to list together in Network Neighborhood should have the same workgroup name). And we'll enter a description of your machine, so anyone on the network can see a bit more about the machine to which they're copying files to or from (or sharing a printer).

Complete the following steps to identify your computer:

1. Right-click **Network Neighborhood** in Windows 95, or **My Network Places** in Windows Me, and choose **Properties** (see Figure 15.5).

Well-Connected Words

In Microsoft networking, a **workgroup** is a collection of computers on your network that all go by the same name. You need to assign your computers to a workgroup when you add them to your network.

Figure 15.5

Right-click Network Neighborhood.

2. Click the **Identification** tab. In the Computer name text box, enter a name for the PC (less than 15 characters and don't use spaces).

3. Enter a workgroup name and click the **OK** button. You can also, but are not required, to add a computer description. If you do, make it something that will uniquely identify the computer on the network (see Figure 15.6).

Figure 15.6

Enter a workgroup name.

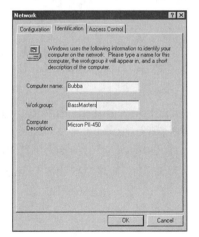

Starting Printer and File Sharing

Your computer won't get much use on a network until you share files. And, if you have a printer connected to your machine, you'll be able to share that, too. If you have your eye on somebody else's printer at your home or office, you can have access to that, too (if they let you).

Let's make your computer ready to share its files for Windows 95 and 98 PCs. And we'll show you the slightly different steps for setting up file and printer sharing for Windows Me at the end of this section.

1. Right-click **Network Neighborhood,** choose **Properties,** and then click the **File and Print Sharing** button (see Figure 15.7).

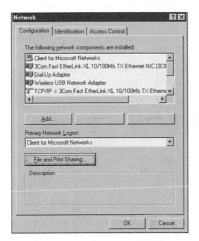

Figure 15.7

Enabling file and printer sharing.

2. Select the **I want to be able to give others access to my files** and **I want to be able to allow others to print to my printer(s)** check boxes. Click the **OK** button on each of the open dialog boxes to close them (see Figure 15.8).

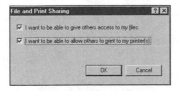

Figure 15.8

Giving access to your files and printers.

3. You may be prompted to insert your Windows operating system CD into your CD drive. Do so, and click the **OK** button (see Figure 15.9).

Figure 15.9

Windows wants your attention, and your OS disk.

If you use Windows Me, here's how to start file and printer sharing:

1. Double-click **My Network Places.**
2. Open the **Home Networking Wizard.**
3. Follow the wizard's prompts, which describe the type of network you are using. Click **Finish** when you're done selecting options in the Home Networking Wizard and restart your computer.

Sharing a Folder

Okay, you've set up the capability for file sharing, but you have yet to share a file. A temporary problem, I assure you. To get the process rolling, you need to tell Windows to share one or more folders. Here's how:

1. Create a new Folder.
2. Right-click the new folder and choose **Sharing** (see Figure 15.10).

Figure 15.10

Select a folder to share.

3. Select **Shared As** and then choose the level of access you want to give. You can let people on your network read your files, give them full access, or require a password. When you're done, click **OK** (see Figure 15.11).

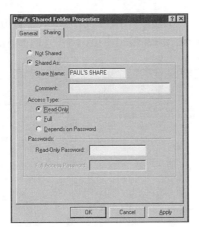

Figure 15.11

Choose whether folks need a password to access your folder.

Setting Up Windows 2000

Let's say you have some Windows 2000 computers in your house or office. It's no big hassle to add them to the network. In fact, it's quite simple because these operating systems were created to be networked.

You'll need to take slightly different steps than you do with more consumer-oriented operating systems, such as Windows 98 and Me. These added steps enhance the security of your network, and they won't take much time.

Adding the Necessary Protocols

As with Windows 95/98/Me, you need to have to install a protocol, which sets guidelines for how computers communicate on your network.

1. Right-click **My Network Places** and choose **Properties.** You can also choose **Start, Settings, Network and Dial-up Connections** (see Figure 15.12).

Figure 15.12

Open Properties for My Network Places.

2. Right-click your network connection, which represents your wireless network adapter, and choose **Properties** (see Figure 15.13).

Figure 15.13

*Open your wireless network
adapter properties.*

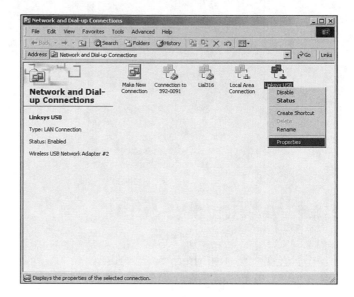

3. You will need the Client for Microsoft Networks, File and Printer sharing for Microsoft Networks, and Internet Protocol (TCP/IP). If you do
not use a router, install the NetBEUI Protocol. To install a client or protocol, choose **Install**, click **Protocol** (or Service), and then click the **Add**
button (see Figure 15.14).

Figure 15.14

*Adding a protocol in
Windows 2000.*

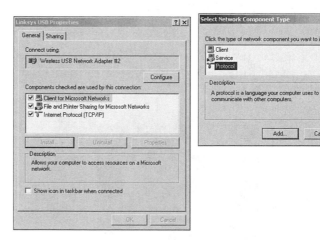

Naming Your Computer

Adding a computer name and workgroup with Windows 2000 is handled in a similar way as you do with Windows 95 and 98.

1. Right-click **My Computer** and select **Properties** (see Figure 15.15).

Figure 15.15

Open My Computer Properties.

2. Select the **Network Identification** tab, and then click the **Properties** button (see Figure 15.16).

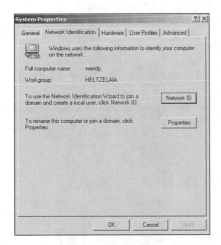

Figure 15.16

Preparing to identify your computer on the network.

3. Add a descriptive, unique computer name, and then enter your workgroup name (see Figure 15.17). Don't add anything to the Domain area unless you are running a Windows server and are instructed to do so by a system administrator (we're assuming that's you, so just leave the Domain area alone).

Figure 15.17

Add a computer name and workgroup name.

Sharing a Folder

Time to make your computer the file-sharing wonder you always knew it could be. Create a folder, or select one that's already on your system, and make it available to everybody on your network.

1. Create a new folder on your hard drive. Right-click the folder and choose **Sharing** (see Figure 15.18).

Figure 15.18

Share a new folder on your new network.

2. Select **Share this folder.**
3. Click the **Permissions** button to change the access to your folder (see Figure 15.19).

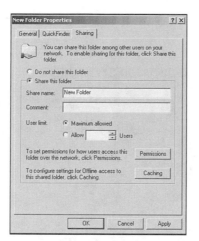

Figure 15.19

Changing the access to your folder.

4. Select whether you want users to have full control or if you only want them to be able to read files. When you're finished, click **OK** (see Figure 15.20).

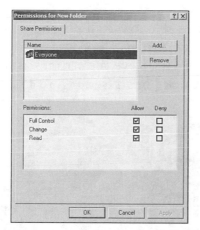

Figure 15.20

Can others on your network have full control of the files you're sharing? It's your call.

Giving Access to Your Computer

Unlike Windows 95/98/Me, each person who wants to access your computer must have a user name and password. Windows 2000 is more security-minded and doesn't like folks mucking around your computer unless they have identification.

1. Choose **Start, Settings, Control Panel.** Open **Users and Passwords.** Select **Add** (see Figure 15.21).

Figure 15.21

The Users and Passwords dialog box shows those who are allowed to access your computer over the network.

2. Enter a name and click **Next.** Enter a password in the next screen and click **Next** again.

3. Choose whether the user will be able to install programs on this computer. If you don't want to all users to install programs over the network, choose **Restricted User.** Otherwise, leave the settings as they are, with the **Standard User** selected. Click **Finish** (see Figure 15.22).

Figure 15.22

Choose Standard or Restricted user access. Restricted users can't install programs on your computer.

Adding a Printer

If you want to share a printer on the network, follow these steps. The basic idea is the same as with versions of Windows 95 or greater.

1. Double-click **My Computer,** and then double-click **Printers** (see Figure 15.23).

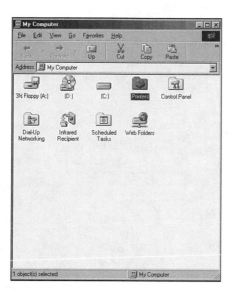

Figure 15.23

Open the Printers dialog box.

2. Open **Add Printer** and follow the prompts. The wizard menu that walks you through installing a printer will differ between versions of Windows, but it's quite straightforward (see Figure 15.24).

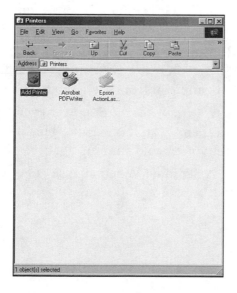

Figure 15.24

Start the Add Printer Wizard.

Watch Out!

Windows 95/98/Me users need to log in (Start, Log in) and use the name and password you have given them at the Windows 2000 machine. If they try and access the Windows 2000 computer without the correct username and password, access won't be allowed. The login menu appears when you start a Windows machine. If you have not logged in with the username and password you need to access the Windows 2000 machine, try this:

1. Select **Start, Log Off.**
2. Click **Yes** when prompted.
3. Enter the correct username and password, then click **OK.**

Troubleshooting Your Setup

Once you get the kinks out of your setup, your network should chug along, without too much upkeep. Getting everything working the first time is the hard part.

Here are a few things to check if you can't get your network up and running:

- First, make sure your data (and power) cables are plugged in and your wireless network adapter is connecting to your access point (usually a wireless network adapter will have a green light or other indicator that it is connecting).

- If you have personal firewall software installed, try quitting it (or changing the settings to allow local area network access). Personal firewall software can block access and can stop you from seeing network resources.

- If you have a router (or router/access point), try power cycling it. That's a slick way of saying, turn it off and turn it on again. This will reset the router and will sometimes get you up and running again.

- An old information technology standby: When all else fails, reboot.

Bet You Didn't Know _____

Internet Connection Sharing (ICS) is a feature introduced in Windows 98 SE and included in each Windows OS that followed. The way you set up ICS differs depending on the operating system you use. ICS turns one of your computers into a server or host. The other computers in your network access the Internet through the computer running this software.

The tricky part is that to share a broadband Internet connection (such as cable or DSL), your computer will need two network adapters. One will connect to your broadband modem, and the other will connect to your network. You will not need a second adapter card if you want to share a dial-up, analog modem. You'll just use your wireless networking adapter, and your network will access the Internet by your modem.

Configuring Internet Connection Sharing isn't exactly a walk in the park, and it varies significantly depending on the operating system you use. Thankfully, Windows Me (through the Home Networking Wizard) and Windows XP (through the Network Setup Wizard) have made the process simpler. You can find out how to share an Internet connection using the Help file that comes with your computer. But frankly, using a router, either built-in to your access point or bought and connected separately, is an easier way to go.

The Least You Need to Know

- ◆ You can set up your network to share an Internet connection, files, and printers using TCP/IP, the communications standard on the Internet.

- ◆ Your computer needs a name to uniquely identify it among the computers in your workgroup. Use the same workgroup name for each computer that you want to associate together in Network Neighborhood.

- ◆ Once you enable file and print sharing, you need to create a folder (or use one you have already) and change its settings so others can access it.

- ◆ If your network does not at first succeed, start by checking simple things, like your wireless network adapters' cable and power connections, and restarting your router or computers.

- ◆ You can share an Internet connection between the computers on your network using software that ships with Windows 98 SE and later. If you can manage it, however, use an inexpensive router, preferably one built into your wireless access point.

Chapter 16

Finding Your Way

In This Chapter

- ◆ Connecting to a GPS receiver
- ◆ Finding a restaurant or movie
- ◆ Making good use of minibrowsers and bookmarks
- ◆ Finding a portal

Recently I was stopped on the street by a well-dressed couple in a late model sedan, on their way to a wedding. They were lost, no doubt about that, and they asked for directions. "Wait just a sec," I told them, my Boy Scout instincts kicking in. I pulled out my PDA and GPS receiver.

I pointed at the little screen on my PDA, which showed their exact location. "See?" said the wife to her husband. She was right, they were on Humbolt Road, not Humbolt Drive.

I entered their destination in a mobile version of MapQuest on the Web, which returned turn-by-turn directions to the VFW hall where they were headed. A well-connected PDA saved the day again. You can have this sort of success, too, with the right tools and wireless Web sites.

Connecting to a GPS Receiver

A *GPS* device can make your PDA or laptop much more useful. Using 24 Defense Department–launched satellites, a receiver can pinpoint your exact position anywhere in the world.

The rub? You need to *buy* a GPS receiver, and that sets you back between $80 and $300. Most run with common AAA batteries and/or plug into a car lighter for juice. And GPS receivers are, of course, naturally designed to be used in mobile situations.

If you're considering a GPS device, you'll likely find one of two setups:

♦ A standalone GPS receiver, with its own small, PDA-like screen, that connects via serial cable to your laptop or PDA. The screen shows your position and offers simple maps to help guide you.

Well-Connected Words

GPS (global positioning system) is a system of 24 satellites, which was launched by the U.S. Department of Defense. A handheld GPS receiver can triangulate signals from three or more satellites and provide your location—including altitude—anywhere in the world.

♦ A bundled package with a less expensive GPS receiver that has no screen, which you connect by cable to a PDA or laptop. These devices are often bundled with software for combining the GPS location capability, with software that displays street directions and databases filled with helpful information for travelers, such as restaurant, gas station, and hotel listings.

You can't assume that any GPS receiver automatically connects to your handheld or PDA of choice. Compatibility is an important consideration here, and it's worth spending some time checking out different vendors' Web sites to find out which devices connect with which. Sellers of relatively inexpensive, handheld GPS manufacturers include Garmin (www.garmin.com) and Magellan (www.magellangps.com).

Typically, you connect a GPS device using the serial port (not the printer port) on your PC, which is probably a laptop—unless you plan to lug your desktop PC around with you on your travels.

Better yet, you can download or purchase software for your PDA or laptop that enables you add maps and provides travel advice while using your GPS device. You can get turn-by-turn directions and even check your speed.

TravRoute (www.travroute.com) sells a version of its GPS receiver and map software for laptops, CoPilot ($399), and Pocket PCs, Pocket CoPilot 2.0, for $299. If you miss a turn, the program even works up the directions from your new location. You can enter an address with your keyboard, but for hands-free use (when you're driving), the software works by voice command. You need a microphone to take advantage of this neat feature.

Watch Out!

Some of the GPS receiver and software options you can purchase will pull power from a laptop serial port. Others need to be plugged into a car's cigarette lighter. Make sure the GPS receiver you buy suits your power situation when traveling before you purchase.

DeLorme's AAA Map'n'Go 7 ($30) can be used with the company's Earthmate GPS receiver ($145) and includes maps and directions as well as 66,000 restaurants, roadside attractions, and accommodations in the United States, Canada, and Mexico (see Figure 16.1).

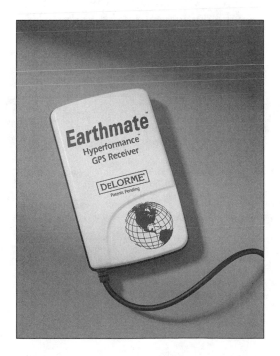

Figure 16.1

Photo of Earthmate® GPS Receiver.

(Photo courtesy of DeLorme, Yarmouth, Maine)

If you already have a GPS receiver that is compatible with your computer, you can purchase mapping software for less than $50 that essentially does the same job as software/GPS receiver bundles.

Take the Internet with You

If you're carrying around a smart phone, you're probably a browsing expert by now. But before we discuss some of the sites you might want to check out when you travel, let's quickly cover some wireless browsing basics.

Most of the sites mentioned here are WAP sites. WAP is the standard used by many smart phones, and some handhelds, to display sites on the Internet. You can view these with a minibrowser (sometimes called a microbrowser) if you have a smart phone. The Mobile Browser from Openwave (formerly Phone. com) is found on many smart phones.

Use a Smart Phone

You typically scroll through your phone's screen (see Figure 16.2), using up and down buttons, to the Internet link on your phone's main screen (it might say Wireless Web or something similar). Launch the minibrowser by selecting it and clicking the **OK** button, or the equivalent of the **Enter** key on your phone.

Figure 16.2

Many phones include a screen that allows you to type in a WAP address.

If the site you want to visit isn't listed on your phone, you might have to enter it. Your phone's minibrowser should show a **Go To** or **Open Location** link in its main screen (you might have to scroll to the end of a screen, select **More,** and press your phone's **OK** or **Enter** key on the keypad to see it.

To input text, press the number keys on your keypad multiple times (press 2 twice for "b," or 8 once for "t," for example).

Synch Up

Okay, let's see, where's the percentage symbol on this &$#*! smart phone? If you send e-mail using your mobile phone, you've probably noticed that the symbol keys we're all used to finding at the top of our PC keyboards are missing on a phone's keypad. You can probably find the symbol you're looking for by searching through a menu on the phone's screen. Here's a trick that's faster though: Pressing the 1 key repeatedly usually brings up symbols (such as @, underscore, and [of course], the dot in dot com).

After you find a site you think you'll use again, make a bookmark. Your mini-browser should have a **Mark** or **Bookmark** selection. (Menus on phones vary widely, but you should have something similar.) Click to mark the site, so you can return to it quickly later. You might be prompted to enter a new name for the bookmark (see Figure 16.3).

Figure 16.3

You can bookmark a site for faster access on your smart phone. Note that menus differ widely by phone, but you should be able to add the site you are viewing to your bookmark list on your phone.

Mobile Surfing with a PDA

If you use a Palm device, such as the Palm VII, to surf the Web, you might need to download a Web clipping application (called a PQA, or Palm Query App) to open sites. We'll point that out where necessary. Pocket PCs use a less feature-filled version of Microsoft's Internet Explorer, called Pocket Explorer. To browse sites using Pocket Explorer, just enter the normal Web address (for example, www.pocketpc.com).

Wireless Travel

Travel sites are a great way to quickly find directions to your destination or get flight arrival information to pick up your significant other—no small matter—on time. Here I provide you with some handy sites for travel, along with their addresses. Truth be told, though, it's usually easier to find these sites, or similar ones set up by your wireless service provider, by clicking the Travel link in your phone or handheld's minibrowser.

One of my favorite uses of a Web phone is instantly checking flight times in an airport. There are, of course, plenty of video screens with arrival and departure information, but they never seem to be where I'm hanging out, such as a newsstand or restaurant. I don't need to search for one again when I'm in a rush because I get up-to-the minute information using trip.com's FlightTracker. If you have a Web phone, try this WAP site: atpgw.com. Every now and then I know the flight delay information before it's announced.

Hotels are another story. When I'm in a cab though, looking for an available hotel when I've been bumped, I'm in no mood to call—and get rejected—hotel by hotel. I look up hotels and check availability on Expedia To Go and then I make the call to book a room. Expedia is listed under the Travel menu in AT&T Wireless phones and works through the MSN Mobile link in Sprint PCS, Verizon, and Nextel Web phones (WAP and Web site: www.expedia. com).

Reading restaurant reviews through Fodors.com (using AvantGo, www. avantgo.com) and then getting directions to them from Mobile MapQuest (www.mapquest.com) is even more fun. Sprint and AT&T make the site available in their Travel menu, or you can bookmark wireless.mapquest.com/wml/. Palm VII users need to download a small application at www.mapquest.com for these features. With all the information available to me on my Web phone, I can say, "Hey cabby, take a right here, and save me two bucks," even though I'm in a city I've never visited before.

Synch Up

Alaska Air and Horizon Air now allow you to check in for domestic flights, as long as you don't need to upgrade, by Web phone or Palm handhelds (with wireless modem). You can find more information on the service at the Alaska Airlines Web site (www.alaskaair.com). You can even check in on the ride to the airport or as you pack up at home. Palm users need to download a small application first, but Web phone users can simply open their minibrowser, select the **Go to** command, and enter the airline's WAP site: wireless.alaskaair.com.

Movies and Entertainment

When I'm traveling I often try to catch a movie. It's fun to see first-run movies in the Big City, and Hollywood.com, dialed up with my phone (wap.hollywood.com), is a fast way to get all the up-to-date listings (see Figure 16.4).

Figure 16.4

Buying movie tickets at Hollywood.com.

So I don't waste my time with a stinker, I check out the service's movie reviews. I might surf over to Hollywood.com to get the thumbs up or down with some entertainment gossip thrown in.

After I've read the review, I get directions right to the theater or click a link to call the theater directly and buy my tickets beforehand. You can also buy movie tickets online using a portal site (see the "One-Stop Surfing: Portals" section later in the chapter).

Wireless Shopping

Shopping on a PDA, for most goods and services, is a bit of a hard sell, because many shopping Web sites don't have WAP versions. Where wireless really comes in handy is when you need to find a shop, and then its location and phone number. What's even better is comparing prices and getting reviews (see Figure 16.5) when you're in the store, so you find the best goods and get a fair price. Almost all Web phones and PDAs come preprogrammed with bookmarks for comparison-shopping. These save you some finger mangling, because entering WAP addresses can be a pain.

Figure 16.5

Catching up on some research at Consumer Reports Electronics, using AvantGo.

A number of sites use numeric product identifiers to find, and compare, products. BarPoint.com (see Figure 16.6) enables you to type in a product's bar code (or a book's ISBN). You can also search by product name (Web and WAP site: www.barpoint.com).

Figure 16.6

Surfing the BarPoint.com WAP site with a smart phone.

Pricegrabber.com is another comparison-shopping site with a numeric twist. You can enter a model number or part number of product you're bargain hunting. If you don't know the part or model number, you can browse by category or search by keyword (Web site: www.pricegrabber.com; WAP site: atpgw.com).

One of the most comprehensive shopping sites around, mySimon, lists product information and pricing from 2,000 online stores, including computers, clothes, flowers, and sporting goods. When you're ready to buy, click a link and you arrive at the merchant's site. mySimon To Go is available by smart phone and PDA (you need to download a small application for PDA use). You can also use this site on BlackBerry handhelds through Motient's eLink service (Web site: www.mysimon.com; WAP site: wap.mysimon.com).

One-Stop Surfing: Portals

When I'm out with clients, just before I pick up the bill, I usually check my bank balance, and if there's time, as I duck around the payphones, I'll check to see if it was a good day for my mutual funds. After I check out a couple headlines and a sports score I've got conversational tidbits to last the evening.

Thankfully, I don't need to browse all over the Internet to find this information. I just use my smart phone (and sometimes an HTML browser on my PDA) to visit a portal. Portals collect links in one place for you, which makes browsing faster. They put news, sports scores, directions, and most of the information you're looking for in one place so that it's all only a link away. When you surf using a tiny screen with limited text-input capability, you'll really find portals handy.

Yodlee is a service that collects the important information from all your online accounts and displays the information on one page that is accessible after using just one password. You don't have to enter your password for each account, and you always see up-to-date information, whether you view from your handheld or from home. There's no synching to do between devices, because all the information is stored online. This service is highly recommended (key in www.yodlee.com). You can even set up your Yodlee account to view your e-mail and headlines from your favorite Web sites.

AOL, MSN (see Figure 16.7), and Yahoo! all offer strong mobile sites, where you can check your e-mail or online calendar plus news, finance, and weather. (AOL, Web and WAP site: www.myaol.com; MSN, Web site: www.msn.com; WAP site: mobile.msn.com; Yahoo! Web site: www.yahoo.com; WAP site: wap.yahoo.com)

Many wireless service providers provide online integration with WAP browsers. Sprint PCS, ALLTEL, and others allow access to your account through the Web, where you can select the sites that appear on your WAP phone and the order in which they appear.

Figure 16.7

Browsing MSN on a Pocket PC.

The Least You Need to Know

- ◆ Got a bad sense of direction? Well, no longer. You can connect a global positioning system (GPS) receiver to your laptop or PDA.

- ◆ You can enter addresses manually in your Web phone's minibrowser, then bookmark sites for fast access later.

- ◆ With a wireless phone or PDA, you can check to see if your flight is on time, find an available hotel, and even check out restaurant reviews.

- ◆ Shopping on a minibrowser can be difficult, but comparison sites help you find the best deals, from different vendors, in a hurry.

- ◆ Portals place all the information you might need in one place, making information convenient to access and easy to read on small screens.

Chapter 17

Beaming with Pride

In This Chapter

- Beaming contacts
- Transferring wireless data between a Pocket PC and Palm
- Beaming record, programs, and documents
- Synching your computer and PDA
- Using a Web site to synch

Mom always said having the latest data was of the utmost importance (Mom was an IT manager at a large bank). And you know something, she was right. That's why this chapter covers synching and beaming data to make sure it's current, no matter where, or on what device, you keep it.

Synching merges the changes you've made, in particular to your calendar, memos, e-mail, and address book, while you're out of the office. This way, information is identical on your PDA and your desktop computer. Beaming enables you to trade information, such as your business card or your expenses, with other PDA users that have infrared ports.

You can synch appointments, expenses, business cards you've traded with other PDA users, and pages from the Web for browsing later. You can even synch and beam programs from one device to another.

Well-Connected Words

Infrared is a beam of light that requires a clear line of site for transmission of data, such as a document sent from one PDA or laptop to another. Many PDAs and laptops use the IrDA (Infrared Data Association) standard for infrared transmission. Note that the Palm OS does not use IrDA.

Some PDAs are able to synch cradle free, using a beam of *infrared* light. That said, synching with the USB cradle that comes with your PDA is quite a bit faster than the infrared capability of your PDA, so slow syncing might offset the advantages of synching wirelessly. And out of the box, most PDAs are unable to communicate with other PDAs that use a different operating system (a Pocket PC and Palm OS PDA, for instance). PDAs are not always ready from the get-go to communicate wirelessly by infrared with PCs, printers, and cell phones; they might need some add-on hardware or software.

Wireless Transfer on the Go

Let's consider a scenario that enables us to explore the most likely ways of transferring data between PDAs, phones, and desktop or laptop computers.

Watch Out!

Keep an eye on your PDA and laptop's battery life when using infrared transmission. The technology is notorious for chewing up power. Try turning off your device's infrared receiving mode to eek out more juice from your batteries.

Say you're attending a conference. At this conference, you want to network (the old-fashioned shake hands and compliment-the-boss variety). You also want to take a high-tech approach, saving paper by beaming records, and transmitting your business card wirelessly from your PDA to the PDAs of folks you meet.

First, let's look at beaming contacts from one PDA to another.

To start, the receiving unit should prepare to receive data (see Figure 17.1). With a Pocket PC, from within Contacts, do the following:

1. Click **Tools.**
2. Click **Receive via Infrared.**

Figure 17.1

Preparing to receive a contact on a Pocket PC.

These two quick steps work for most Pocket PC applications when you're ready to receive data.

Palm OS handhelds are ready to receive beamed data by default. But if you have trouble, make sure you're set up to receive infrared data:

1. Select the **Applications** icon. (It looks like a little house.)
2. Click the **Preferences** icon.
3. Select the **General** drop-down menu from the upper right.
4. Click the down-pointing arrow next to **Beam Receive** and choose **On.**

To send a contact via infrared from one Palm to another, take these quick and painless steps. It's a good idea, before you leave on a business trip, to enter your own information into your address book, and select it as your business card for trading later.

1. Click the **Address Book** button (it looks like a phone).
2. Create a new contact and enter your information.
3. Click the **Menu** icon.
4. Choose **Select Business Card** (see Figure 17.2).
5. Click **Yes** when asked if you want to make the contact your business card.

Figure 17.2

Selecting a business card on a Palm OS handheld.

To beam your new card, just follow these steps:

1. Click the **Address** icon in the Applications panel.
2. Select an address from your list of contacts.
3. Click the **Menu** icon on your Palm (in the lower left).
4. Select **Beam Business Card** (see Figure 17.3).

Synch Up

You can also beam your business card by simply pressing and holding your **Address Book** button.

Figure 17.3

Beaming a business card.

To transfer a contact from one Pocket PC to another, follow these steps:

1. Select the contact.
2. From the **File** menu, select **Send and Receive.**

Beaming Other Data

You're not just limited to beaming contacts. No sir. You can send all kinds of files wirelessly, including database records, appointments, even programs you've downloaded and want to send to a friend.

You can transfer appointments (see Figure 17.4), programs, spreadsheet and word processing files (see Figure 17.5), and all sorts of other documents. Palm devices are usually ready to receive by default (but you shouldn't be working in a program if you're getting ready to receive). If you have a Pocket PC and want to receive a file, choose **Tools, Receive via Infrared.**

Most often, you select the file or program you want to send, and then tap the **Tools** menu (with a Pocket PC) or the **Menu** button (on Palm). The **Send via Infrared** or **Beam** menu choice comes up onscreen. You can beam all sorts of files: a memo, your resumé, or anything else you need to share and beam that while you are networking.

Figure 17.4

Sharing a calendar event with a colleague, care of Palm OS.

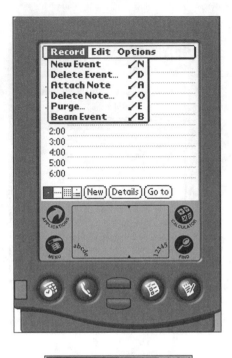

Figure 17.5

Take that: an Excel spreadsheet sent via infrared.

Making Friends: Pocket PCs and Palm Handhelds

Transmitting contacts and other data wirelessly works great if the people you want to communicate with all use handhelds with the same operating systems.

But as is often the case, things just aren't that simple. What if, considering our scenario again, everybody at the conference you attend has different kinds of handhelds?

You can actually beam contacts from a Palm to a Pocket PC, but you first need to purchase software to handle the job. Peacemaker is one such application you can install on a PocketPC (www.conduits.com/ce/peacemaker). In fact, some PDAs, such as the Compaq iPaq, ship with this helpful utility in its software bundle.

Got a Palm? You can install SyncTalk, a program that works on Palm and Pocket PC handhelds (www.synctalk.com). Now hit the big after-conference party, and get ready for some wireless networking.

Synching Up Your PDA or Phone

After you return from your trip, or better yet, when you get back to your hotel room, it's a good idea to synch up your contacts with your home or office computer.

Typically, you'll use the cradle that comes with your PDA (see the Sony CLIE in Figure 17.6). Older cradles use serial cables; newer cradles use USB cables for faster connections. You might even think about buying a separate synching cable (without the cradle so it's less bulky and easier to pack), which usually runs about $20.

Figure 17.6

A Sony CLIE, in its cradle, ready to synchronize data with a desktop PC.

You won't use a cradle to go make an Internet connection through your computer (it's possible but quite tricky). Before your next trip, however, you can synch up to download Web pages and other information to take with you.

After you drop your PDA into its cradle, synching is usually a one-button affair. But because we're primarily interested in wireless technology, let's say you left your cradle at home, and you want to synch up with a laptop that has an infrared port.

First, make sure your computer is ready to receive infrared data. For these steps, we assume you are using a current version of the Palm or Pocket PC operating system. If you are using an older version of your PDA's operating system, you can find help (and the downloads you need) at Palm or Handspring's Web sites (www.palm.com, www.handspring.com) or Microsoft's Pocket PC site (www.pocketpc.com). Each offers guidance, screenshots, and links to the files you need.

Synching with infrared can be a little confusing. For instance, Windows 95 needs an infrared driver you can download from www.microsoft.com/windowsce. And Palm operating systems earlier than the 3.5 operating system need the Enhanced Infrared Update, which you can download from Palm's support site at www.palm.com/support/. The Handspring site can point you to BeamSync, a small, free program for synching up via Infrared for Handspring PDAs that use Palm OS 3.1, which does not include support for infrared.

Synch Up

What if you don't have an infrared port on your PC? You can always add one (for about $70). Extended Systems (www.extendedsystems.com) sells the XTNDAccess IrDA adapter, which enables you to trade data between computers with infrared ports as well as send documents wirelessly to a printer.

Whew. Okay, are you still with me?

Note that your desktop computer must be set up to send and receive via infrared before you can start. Macs should be ready by default. In Windows 95/98, select **Start, Control Panel,** and double-click **Infrared.** Click the **Options** tab and select **Enable infrared communication on** (see Figure 17.7). Remember the COM port that Windows is using. Select **OK** twice to close the open dialog boxes.

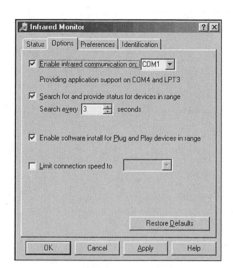

Figure 17.7

Enabling infrared support in Windows 98.

Here's how to synch up a Pocket PC and computer using infrared:

1. Make sure your infrared ports on your computer and Pocket PC are lined up.
2. Click **Start, Programs, Connections,** and choose **IR ActiveSync.**

Here's how to synch a Palm with your Windows PC:

1. Windows users should right-click the **HotSync manager** icon in the system tray (next to the clock in the bottom right) and select **Setup.** Then click the **Local** tab. Choose the COM port that Windows is using and click **OK** (see Figure 17.6).
2. Click the HotSync icon in your system tray and make sure **Local Serial** is selected.
3. On your Palm handheld, select the **HotSync icon** in the Applications launcher.
4. Select **Local.**
5. Click the **pop-up menu** under the HotSync icon.
6. Select **IR to a PC/Handheld.**
7. Line up the infrared ports between the Palm and the computer.
8. Click the **HotSync** icon, and the data will transfer, wirelessly. Neat, huh?

Here's how to synch a Palm with your Mac:

1. Double-click the **HotSync Manager icon** to launch the HotSync Manager.

2. From the Serial Port Settings tab, choose **As fast as possible** from the Speed pop-up menu and **Infrared Port** from the Port pop-up menu (see Figure 17.8).

3. On your Palm handheld, select the **HotSync** icon in the Applications launcher.

4. Select **Local.**

5. Click the pop-up menu under the HotSync icon.

6. Select **IR to a PC/Handheld.**

7. Line up the infrared ports between the Palm and the computer.

8. Click the **HotSync** icon, and the data will transfer, wirelessly.

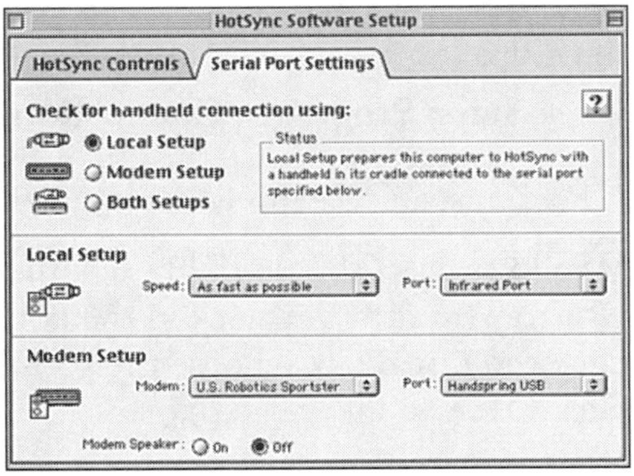

Figure 17.8

Setting up a Mac to synch via infrared.

Synch Through a Web Site

Let's get back to our hypothetical conference. You're about to catch a keynote speaker and want to check your calendar to make sure your afternoon is free. You might keep your calendar on your phone, or maybe it's on your PDA. If your calendar is on your phone, laptop, or PDA, you're all set.

If you need a calendar to which more than one person needs access to enter appointments, consider keeping the data online. That way, everyone can see the appointments from wherever they are, and the schedule is always up to date.

If you can establish a wireless connection with your mobile phone, PDA, or laptop, you could synch your calendar up on a Web site, including mobile.yahoo.com and the MyPalm portal site (my.palm.com). BlackBerry handhelds are especially handy at this kind of task, because they stay in synch, wirelessly, with the Outlook or Lotus Notes server back at the home office (see Chapter 10, "Wireless E-Mail Devices," for more on BlackBerry handheld pagers). You can make adjustments to your schedule from wherever you are, and folks back at the office can note the changes.

Synch Up

Your smart phone might be able to synchronize with your desktop computer's personal information manager (PIM), such as Microsoft Outlook, using a cable or cradle. The Palm–OS based smartphones from Samsung and Kyocera will synch with PIMs as will the Ericsson R380. Check with your phone's maker: You might be able to synch up your phone's calendar, to-do list, and e-mail.

Of course, if you're on your own, the best way to keep your calendar is to synch up often, using your wireless or USB connection.

The Least You Need to Know

- You can beam all kinds of files, including business cards and programs, using an infrared beam of light, from one PDA to another.
- You can send data from a Pocket PC to a Palm, or vice versa, if you have the right software.
- To keep your data current on all your wireless devices (and your computer), synch up often.
- Synching up wirelessly takes some effort but is handy on the road if you don't want to carry a cradle for synching your PDA and computer. See Chapter 18, "Wireless Road Tricks," for more on synching up with the MyPalm (and other) Web sites.

Wireless Road Tricks

In This Chapter

◆ Send a fax from wherever you are

◆ One synch for the road

◆ Wireless synch up

◆ Browse offline

I have an uncle who is also a great psychic. He predicted the 1973 energy crisis, and, interestingly, the Pocket PC. But his greatest prediction was this: "Nephew," he told me, "one day you will work from wherever you want. You'll just need the right tools."

My clairvoyant uncle was on target again. Sign up for a free fax service here, plug in a wireless network card there. Soon you'll have just about everything you need to pull off the mobile office.

Not everybody works on the run, however. Because the fax is still a business standard, you might need to turn the notes you have on your phone, PDA, or laptop into a fax your co-workers can share at a meeting.

We'll look at trading a seemingly hi-tech USB cradle in favor of a wireless add-on card that will enable you to synch up over a corporate or home network.

You might, on occasion, leave your wireless devices behind, but you'll still need your contact and schedule information.

In this chapter we look at a few Web sites that help you synchronize your PDA or desktop with a Web site, so you can view your schedule and contacts over the Internet, anywhere you have access to a Web browser.

My crazy uncle never even saw that one coming.

Sending a Fax

Sending faxes can make your wireless equipment much more useful. A fax machine is another way to print documents for mobile workers who don't have access to a printer, and a fax can also be used to communicate with fellow workers, clients, and anyone else who needs a printout. When you don't have a printer, or your recipient doesn't have e-mail, faxing is the way to go.

In most cases, you can send faxes using a PDA or laptop. In addition, some Web-based services can help you fax from all sorts of wireless devices.

Here are a few ways you can work with faxes when you're out of the office:

◆ You can use an e-mail-to-fax Web site, which converts the e-mail you send into fax format and routes it to the fax machine you choose.

◆ You can receive, and view a fax, using a Web browser that displays the fax as a graphic on your laptop.

◆ You can use a PDA or smart phone to view information about a fax, such as the sender and document size, and then forward the fax to a fax machine. You probably will not view the fax on the screen of the wireless device.

Services Offering Fax Capability

Choosing the best way to send a fax depends on your hardware. A wireless fax modem and a laptop can provide you with the greatest number of possibilities to send and receive.

- Among the Web-based fax services available, eFax (www.efax.com) is one of the most popular and easiest to use. The service provides you with a fax number that receives faxes sent to you and stores them online. You visit the eFax Web site, log in, and then view the fax or print it out. You can also send a fax, using the service, from a laptop. This is a handy way to fax from just about any device with an HTML browser.

- OmniSky (www.omnisky.com) provides fax service for Palm OS hand-helds, such as the Handspring Visor line and Palms. You select a fax number from your address book, and it appears in the address field of the message you're faxing. Click **Send** and you're off.

- If you connect your Web phone to your laptop, examine the choices pro-vided by your phone (service varies widely). Some providers, including Voicestream, offer an add-on service that enables you to send faxes using a PC Card modem, which transmits the data over a GSM network.

- You can send faxes as an e-mail attachment if your wireless handheld uses the GoAmerica (www.goamerica.com) service. GoAmerica offers wireless data services for about $10 to $30 a month, based on use, for Palm OS handhelds, Pocket PCs, and BlackBerry two-way pagers.

Backing Up Data

Both Palm OS and Pocket PCs save files to your desktop computer when you place your PDA in its cradle and synch. Synch often and synch early, the saying goes, to protect your valuable data.

But what about when you're on the road?

One way to get the job done is to use a *Web portal*. Several companies allow you to upload your schedule, contacts, and notes to the Web. By doing this, you get two benefits:

- The ability to check your data even if you don't have your PDA with you.

Well-Connected Words

A **Web portal** is a site on the Internet that aggregates all sorts of content into one place. In a Web portal, you typically find free e-mail accounts, news, sports, entertainment, stocks, and other information you usually search for all over the Web. Increasingly, Web portals are including tools for synching up data from PDAs and Web phones.

♦ The security of a remote backup, which you can access from anywhere you can make an Internet connection.

Yahoo! users who own VII, V, and III Palm handhelds can synch their calendar, address books, and notepad information by downloading and installing an application called Intellisync at mobile.yahoo.com (look for a PDA link which will take you to the Intellisnyc download area). Check out Intellisync for Yahoo! in Figure 18.1.

Figure 18.1

Preparing to use Intellisync for Yahoo!, which compares the data on your PDA or desktop organizer and updates a Web site with your information, such as your contacts, to-do list, and schedule.

You can synch Palm OS handhelds (including Visors, of course) at the MyPalm Web site (my.palm.com). Just sign up for a free account at the site. Online, you can enter your appointments, contacts, even important birthdays. You need to download a small application, called XTNDConnect, from the MyPalm Web site for synching the site and your handheld (see Figure 18.2).

Figure 18.2

Synching online with MyPalm.

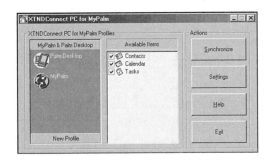

But what if you don't use a Palm device? You can check out a service called FusionOne (www.fusiononec.com) that works with both mobile phones and PDAs, including Pocket PCs, enabling you to synch from one device and retrieve from another.

Watch Out!

If you use a Palm device, it's a good idea to back up your data before synching with a Web portal. For example, to backup your appointments in Palm Desktop, click the **Date** icon, and then choose **File, Export,** and enter a name for your Date Book Archive. Finish up by clicking the **Export** button. Follow these steps for your addresses, to-do list, and memos.

If you use a Pocket PC, you can back up your data this way. On your PC, double-click the **ActiveSync** icon in your system tray (in the bottom-right corner of the screen). Choose **Tools, Backup/Restore.** Select **Full** or **Incremental backup** (just the data that has changed since your last backup). To finish, click **Back Up Now,** and select **OK.**

Portable Wireless Networking

When you're at home or the office, a fast and simple way to synch is with a wireless network card. You attach the card to your PDA or laptop, then synch your files and data. The same wireless network card can be used to connect to both your home or office local area network (as long as they both use the same wireless networking standard, such as 802.11b). You can even connect at some coffee shops, hotels, and airport lounges that offer wireless LAN access. And if the LAN you connect to has fast Internet access, you'll be ready to surf and check e-mail.

Synch Up

You can share text files between your desktop and Palm VII or WAP-capable phone using Xdrive Plus (plus.xdrive.com). The service is an online storage site where you can read, share, and delete your files using your wireless device. The cost is $5 for 25MB of data, and you can add 25MB blocks for $3 more a month.

For about $300, Xircom sells 802.11b wireless LAN (local area network) cards for PDAs, including Handspring Visors and the Palm m500. You can use the cards to connect PDAs to your home or office network. They can also be used to connect PDAs to a desktop or laptop computer for transferring data or synching.

Proxim sells the Harmony OpenAir *CompactFlash* Card, which allows Pocket PCs with *compact flash cards* to connect to wireless home and office networks. The card uses both the HomeRF or OpenAir wireless networking standards. (Note: These are not compatible with 802.11b products.)

Well-Connected Words

The **CompactFlash** socket built into some PDAs (such as many Pocket PCs) can be used to connect PDAs to wireless modems, mobile phones, and local network adapters (see www.socketcom.com). The CompactFlash card, connected to a cable, slides into a CompactFlash socket on your PDA. CompactFlash cards are often used with PDAs and other small electronics, such as digital cameras, for removable storage. A CompactFlash card is about one-third the size of a PC Card.

Taking It with You (Offline Browsing)

Lots of Web sites use AvantGo (see Figure 18.3), a service that formats Web sites so that they can be viewed on PDAs. The service offers versions of Web sites, called channels, with text and simple graphics that can be viewed on playing-card-size PDA screens. You can synch up a PDA and view offline or synch wirelessly if you have a modem.

The AvantGo application offers channel browsing through its own format for serving up pages, rather than HTML (the lingua franca of the Web) or WAP (which many mobile phones use to surf sites set up for WAP browsing).

You can use the AvantGo application to load up your favorite sites and view them offline when you travel. Your data might not be as fresh as it would be if you connected wirelessly, but it's still useful when you have wireless down time.

This free service works with many Palm, Pocket PCs, and WAP phones. The software synchs with computers using Windows 98 or later as well as Mac-intoshes. (Palm-only support, however, is offered for the Mac.)

Synch Up

If you want to check out the wireless Web before you buy a phone or PDA, take a look at the WAP (Wireless Application Protocol) Emulator at www.gelon.net. The site launches a Web-emulator that looks like a smart phone. After it's launched you can use the emulator to jump around a site, just as if you were logging on using a mobile phone. You can check out the display from a handful of different Web-capable phones. WAP is a standard that provides Internet access to phones and other handheld devices.

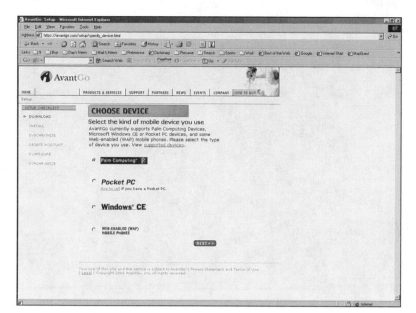

Figure 18.3

Preparing for offline surfing with AvantGo.

You can also grab up-to-date Web information when you connect a wireless modem to your PDA. A mobile phone, connected by serial cable to your handheld, can also do the trick. Check with your cell phone manufacturer to see if it offers a cable that can connect to your PDA.

To sign up for AvantGo, open your browser on your computer and go to www.avantgo.com. Select from hundreds of available channels, and download the AvantGo application for your PDA (see Figure 18.4). If you use a mobile phone for browsing, open your WAP browser and head on over to wap. avantgo.com.

Handhelds aren't the only wireless devices used for offline browsing. If you plan a big trip soon, think about taking some offline Web pages with you. Just connect your laptop to the Internet, and use Internet Explorer on a Mac or PC to download Web pages to your hard drive.

Here's the basic idea. From Internet Explorer, create a bookmark (IE calls bookmarks "Favorites") of a site you want to view offline. Right-click the **Favorite,** and select **Make Available Offline** (the exact wording might vary depending on the version of IE you're using).

Figure 18.4

Selecting channels to view with AvantGo.

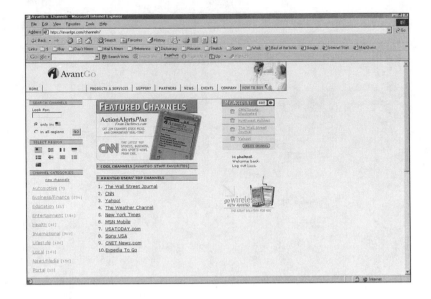

If you use a Mac …

1. Click **Favorites, Subscribe,** and click **Customize.**

2. Click the **Offline** tab and select the option **Download site for offline browsing.**

3. Then click **Options,** select the content you want to view offline, and click **OK.**

4. From the Favorites menu, choose **Update Subscriptions.**

5. From the File menu, select **Work Offline.** Then select the Web site you want to see from the Favorites menu.

Where to from Here?

That futuristic commercial used to say you'd fax from the beach. By today's standards, that idea seems almost quaint. Not only can you fax from anywhere you want, you can pretty much use any wireless device you want.

Now that you've got some information on services that can help you fax and browse offline for free, it's time to get on the Web and try them out. Avant-Go, in particular, is a fun and useful tool that helps you get more out of your wireless device when you travel.

Synching up often can help you avert the disaster of a PDA that has lost all its power. Occasionally synch up online for the win-win of being able to access your data off the Web and the security of knowing you have another backup.

Viva la free wireless Web!

The Least You Need to Know

- ◆ You can send and receive faxes on the go, using a wireless modem or mobile phone connected to a laptop.
- ◆ You can also send text-based faxes using PDAs, Web phones, and (some) two-way pagers. Some PDAs, with an add-on service, can receive faxes and print them out later.
- ◆ You can synch up contacts, appointments, tasks, and notes using Web sites that you can access even when you don't have your wireless device with you. All you need is a connection to the Internet and a browser.
- ◆ Browsing offline can be a fun way to stay on top of things. You can also use offline browsing for speedy browsing, because pages are stored on your laptop or PDA (and don't need to be retrieved over the Web while you're not connected).

Chapter 19

Dealing with Incompatibility

In This Chapter

- Getting your wireless devices on the same page
- Put a Web browser on your PDA
- Working with Word and Excel on a Palm
- Web sites with know how

Like the affable town doctor who befriends a Hatfield and a McCoy, the Internet helps make things that are usually incompatible talk to each other.

You can send e-mail on your PC, and your pal can read it on her iMac. An Excel spreadsheet e-mailed to a co-worker bypasses a hard drive that can't read your floppy disks. Using wireless devices provides the added benefit of mobility, and enables you to work on documents (and e-mail and appointments) from wherever you are.

Of course, the Internet hasn't figured out how to cure all evils. Pocket PCs still aren't speaking to Palms. And smart phones won't give the time of day to your laptop.

Here we'll look at hardware and software that you can buy or download to make your devices play well together and with others. It's just common courtesy. Your devices don't have to play Hatfield and McCoy. Here's how to get them to settle down and get to work.

Wireless Communication Breakdown

You want to enter information (a business card) on one device (a PDA) and read it on another (your desktop PC). If those devices aren't set up to talk to each other, you could have some serious difficulty transferring files and keeping everything straight.

Here's a list of things you probably want to do with your wireless devices:

- ◆ View files from your desktop computer on your PDA.
- ◆ Transfer files from a handheld device to a desktop computer, laptop, or another PDA.
- ◆ Print files from a PDA or laptop over a wireless network.

These day-to-day tasks can be drudgery without the right tools. Here are a few ways to get around various incompatibilities:

- ◆ Download an inexpensive utility that enables you to take a peek at, and more importantly, edit documents even if you don't have the software with which they were created.
- ◆ Send files wirelessly over the Internet or a local area network (LAN).
- ◆ Because many files can't be printed directly from a PDA, you can use a software add-on to send files by infrared to your printer. You might also need a bit of hardware for the printer, but it won't break the bank. You can purchase software for about $20, and a hardware printer infrared adapter for about $70, from www.bachmannsoftware.com.

Bet You Didn't Know _____

The Pocket PC operating system is also called Windows CE 3. Devices that use older versions of the operating system, such as Windows CE 2.0 and CE 1.0, are still useful for linking up addresses and sending appointments and reminders. Software written for earlier versions of the OS is likely to run on Pocket PCs, but Pocket PC applications don't run on older versions of Windows CE. Handheld PCs from Microsoft, which feature tiny keyboards and are now aimed at commercial and industrial users, also use Windows CE. Handheld and Pocket PCs use different types of processors, so often a program written for one doesn't work with the other. Because most Windows CE computers are Pocket PCs these days, the incompatibility between the two is less of an issue.

Browsing for Answers

On laptops, PDAs, and smart phones, you can't always see what you can get. Pocket PCs view pages differently from smart phones. And the Palm's method of "Web clipping" works differently, too.

Most smart phones, as we know, use a WAP browser, which is limited to viewing pages written for WAP, a tiny portion of the Web at large. That's not to say the WAP sites out there, nearly two million of them, aren't useful. It's just that they can't read every site you might like to view.

To expand what PDAs can view, Palm and Handspring users can download HTML browsers from www.palm.com and www.handspring.com, which have abundant, and well-managed pages, linking to software for the Palm OS. This enables Palm OS users to view many more sites, though a bit slowly, because HTML (regular Web) sites are more graphic intensive than Web clipping sites. An HTML Web browser can be very handy if you have a wireless modem or connect to a smart phone.

Pocket PC's Internet Explorer views most Web pages as you'd see them if you were browsing from your desktop computer with Netscape or Internet Explorer. However, there are some common Web technologies the pocket version of Internet Explorer does not support, including Java (small, downloadable, often multimedia programs you find on the Web).

Keep in mind, however, that many wireless network service providers charge for usage. If you browse the Internet using an HTML browser, rather than a WAP browser or Palm's Web-clipping applications, you'll be downloading more data and potentially paying a lot for it.

Wireless service providers OmniSky (www.omnisky.com) and GoAmerica (www.goamerica.com) offer software that makes browsing more efficient by removing graphics and using data compression. Compression encodes data to reduce its size, which gives the appearance of browsing on a higher speed connection.

Synch Up

Want to use your Palm to browse the Web? If you don't want to pay for a wireless modem, you can connect all sorts of cell phones to Palm OS handhelds with cables from this company: Purple Data Cables (www.pcables.com). Purple Data also sells cables to connect Palm and Handspring PDAs to GPS receivers. The cables cost about $39, and you need to download a browser, which you can get free from Eudora at www.eudora.com. Handspring sells a browser for the Palm OS, called Blazer, for about $20. You can find other HTML browsers for Palm OS at www.download.com or the Handspring or Palm Web sites.

If you can't use an HTML browser on your device, the best bet is to use your WAP browser or Web clipping software for quick tasks such as:

- Checking bank balances
- Finding directions
- Grabbing a weather report
- Perusing news updates, stock quotes, and movie listings

Software That Excels in Conversions

The Pocket PC is designed to work with Microsoft Office software, such as Excel, PowerPoint, and Word (see Figure 19.1). In fact, Pocket PCs ship with mini versions of all three built into the operating system. But what if you use a Palm OS handheld?

Figure 19.1

Editing a file using Pocket Word.

Many utilities are available (check out Download.com, shown in Figure 19.2) that enable you to work on Office documents using a Palm. Some are free; others offer a free trial period after which you can pay a registration fee if you decide to keep the program.

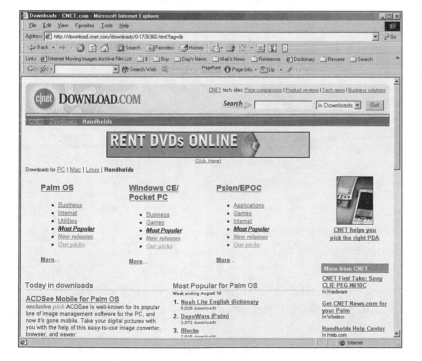

Figure 19.2

The Download.com Web site, where you can find file converters for your handheld.

Check out the following if you need to take your documents with you:

♦ To read and edit Excel and Word documents, you might try Quickoffice from Cutting Edge Software (see Figure 19.3). Quickoffice offers light versions of the Office spreadsheet and word processing programs, which can handle basic data input and editing. The programs even come with simple spreadsheet templates, such as expenses, loan tracking, a checkbook, and a time card. You can buy Quickoffice for about $30, which includes the little word processing and spreadsheet programs, as well as a chart-making tool. The catch? You need a version of Microsoft Word (version 5.0 or later) on your desktop computer.

Figure 19.3

Using Quickoffice to edit a Microsoft Word file on a Palm OS handheld.

♦ Documents to GO by Dataviz, like Quickoffice, enables you to work on Word and Excel files on the Palm OS. The software has the added benefit of working with Microsoft PowerPoint files ($65).

♦ Taking a more focused approach, WordSmith from Blue Nomad (about $30) enables you to write and edit Microsoft Word documents on Palm OS handhelds. Users give it high marks for its full support of external keyboards, including the ability to use menus without having to tap the screen. Note: You can purchase a keyboard for your PDA, but at extra expense—$70 or more at www.bluenomad.com.

Realistically, it's hard to take an Excel spreadsheet and make it useful on a small PDA screen. And serious editing of a word processing document without a keyboard is pretty much out of the question. Keep your documents simple, and choose tasks you can handle on the road, like maintaining a simple spreadsheet or a small PowerPoint presentation, so you don't have to lug around your laptop. When you simplify, you avoid conversion headaches, including out of place characters, wacky formatting, and documents that are just too big to read on a small screen. Going from a PC to PDA, then back to PC again can really throw off formatting. Again, keep it simple.

Web Sites with Know-How

If your problems are mostly related to making your computers talk to each other, these Web sites can help. Whether you need Macs and PCs to converse over a wireless network or you need to find ways to connect various devices to the Internet, you can find answers at these sites:

> ◆ **HomeNetHelp.com (www.homenethelp.com).** This site is smart, insightful, and clearly written. HomeNetHelp.com is a great starting place for anyone interested in networking, wireless or otherwise (see Figure 19.4).

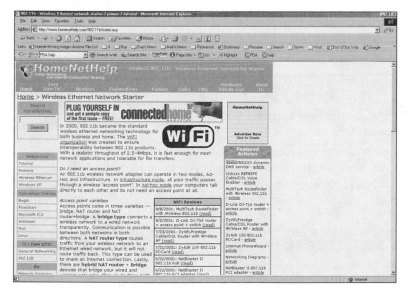

Figure 19.4

Getting the straight dope on tricky wireless networking questions at HomeNethelp.com.

◆ **MacWindows (www.macwindows.com).** This site is a must-read for anyone trying to get Macs and PCs working on the same team (see Figure 19.5). The site is slightly more technical than most we refer you to, but networking computers from different operating systems is no walk in the park. MacWindows provides great advice on mixing the two operating systems over a wireless network.

Figure 19.5

End the feud: Bone up on making Mac and Windows work together.

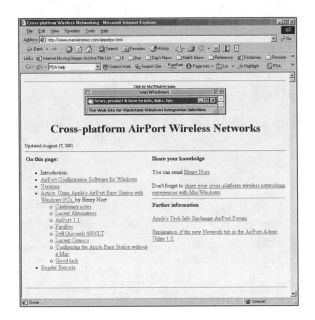

Synch Up

Sure, you can view documents you create on your desktop on your PDA—but you need to synch up and purposefully copy them onto your Palm or Pocket PC. But what happens if you forget a file at home?

AlertWire's Omni is a program that enables you to use a Web browser on any device—including a WAP browser on a smart phone, a BlackBerry handheld, or a PDA, to connect to your computer wirelessly. Like other remote access software (such as PCAnywhere and LapLink), you can use Omni to manage files, open documents, and even check e-mail that's on your desktop. The service fits whatever you want to view to a format that is appropriate for the screen on which you're viewing it, whether it's a WAP phone or a PDA. You can try the program free for 30 days at www.alertwire. com. After that, the service costs about $10 a month.

◆ **Smart Computing (www.smartcomputing.com).** This site offers plenty of great tips on getting PDAs connected to the Internet and covers, in detail, both Pocket PCs and Palm OS handhelds. The site also features news and reviews of all types of hardware and software, and its PDA coverage is top-notch.

The Least You Need to Know

◆ You can get your wireless devices talking to each other, with the right (inexpensive) hardware add-ons and software.

◆ Downloading an HTML browser to your PDA gives you a fuller picture of the Web when you travel. You get greater access to the Web and graphics but lose some speed benefits provided by WAP pages and Web clipping (if you use a Palm handheld).

◆ Since wireless service providers often charge for usage (rather than offering unlimited use, as with most dial-up Internet services), viewing Web sites with an HTML browser on your PDA might be costly. Make sure you know what you're being billed for before you starting surfing the Web wirelessly.

◆ There are plenty of conversion programs and editors that enable you to view or edit documents you use every day, taking a word processing document or spreadsheet, for instance, on the road with your PDA.

Part 4   Making the Connection

Does your phone have to be full of junk e-mail? Does your wireless Web connection need to be fleet? In this part, you'll find loads of tips and advice on keeping the connections you've established earlier in the book running like a champ.

Finally, we give our predictions on up-and-coming technology. Should you wait for faster wireless networks? A phone that can play videos? We'll give you a heads-up on the wireless equipment you'll be using soon.

Chapter 20

Taking Precautions

In This Chapter

- Keeping your PDA secure
- Watching out for power problems
- Avoiding wireless network slowdowns
- Checking coverage before you go
- Protecting your PDA (and other wireless devices) from spam

My father recently had his smart phone eaten by a pack of dogs. He returned to his truck after a visit with a friend to see just a torn-up leather case waiting for him—with no phone.

He took his empty case into the local reseller where he bought it. He showed the salesman the empty case and said, "You'll never believe what happened, but …" and the salesman cut him off, saying, "A dog ate your cell phone. It happens all the time." They replaced his phone, no charge.

Could this happen to you? You bet. Will you be prepared? Definitely. Your data will be safe and secure, because you read this chapter, where we'll look at ways to be ready for action when you take your data wireless.

You won't catch a boy scout hiking the trail without waterproof matches or a Swiss army officer hitting the Alps without his trusty knife. You, too, can be prepared, with a few of these tips under your belt.

Protection with Surge Suppression

All your wireless savvy will lead to naught if a power surge zaps your PDA during a recharge. Don't give up hope: You can protect your PDA with an inexpensive device that offers surge suppression.

The Fellowes laptop surge protector costs you about $25 and offers a $50,000 equipment guarantee if it fails (see Figure 20.1). You can pick one up at most electronics and office supply stores. Along the same lines, the Kensington Smartsocket ($15) includes a phone splitter, so you can plug in your modem and the phone at the same time. These are also widely available at electronics and office supply stores.

Figure 20.1

The Fellowes laptop surge protector for power and phone.

Move the Microwave

If you use, or are shopping for, wireless networking equipment you probably know that most wireless networks operate on the 2.4GHz frequency, like some other electronics, including microwaves.

If you have a microwave near your wireless networking equipment, and it appears to be interfering with and sometimes slowing your network when the microwave is in operation, consider moving it to another room.

Most home networking products now offer means to avoid interference, so you probably won't have any problems. But if you see a noticeable change when the microwave is operating, the easiest way to stop the problem is to move the microwave.

Find a Replacement Antenna

Accidentally snap off the antenna on your smart phone? No problem. You can contact your vendor for a replacement. Purchase a third-party antenna and you can save yourself some money. You can find replacement antennas at many stores, including on the Web at iGo.com.

Keep in mind, however, that taller is not necessarily better. The length of an antenna is carefully matched to the frequencies it handles. That's why 800MHz phones—generally analog—have extendible antennas and 1,900MHz PCS phones do not.

Two-Way Paging Tip

Many two-way paging devices, including the BlackBerry handheld and Motorola two-way pagers, use the Motient, Cingular Wireless (see Figure 20.2), SkyTel, or WebLink Wireless network. Before you take off, check to see if your provider offers coverage in the area to which you're headed. If not, take another device with you, such as your smart phone or laptop.

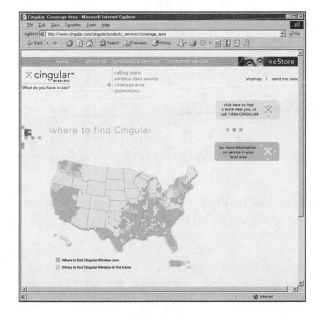

Figure 20.2

Checking out two-way paging coverage at Cingular Wireless.

Here's where to find a coverage map before you go:

- Motient (www.motient.com)
- Cingular Wireless (www.cingular.com)
- SkyTel (www.skytel.com)
- WebLink Wireless (www.weblinkwireless.com)

The Plane

Boeing is working with three major airlines—United, Delta, and American—to create a wireless, two-way broadband service (called Connexion) on commercial planes. The plan is to outfit about 1,500 planes with wireless Internet access through satellite. The service is expected to be available in 2002.

For now, the Airfone (www.airfone.com) by GTE offers 9.6kbps data and fax connections. Charges are high, though, about $4 to connect plus $4 a minute for voice and fax. Data calls run about $2 a minute with no connection charge.

While we wait for airborne broadband, you're probably best off answering your e-mail on your PDA or laptop offline when you fly. When you get on the ground, just fire up your wireless connection, and send all your mail in a batch. Sometimes a little time offline can be just what you need to take care of business.

Get a Bathroom or ATM Finder App

Heading to the big city? If you use a Palm VII, why not download a small Web-clipping application for your handheld that can help you find the important things in life.

Where-2-Go is a Public Restrooms Locator (PRL) application that can help you find the best restrooms in Manhattan. You can download the application at www.rovenet.com.

When you visit the Palm site, you can also find an ATM locator, from MasterCard. It's actually more helpful than a single bank's ATM locator, because MasterCard is accepted at quite a few ATMs. It also provides the locations of money machines that accept cards that are part of the Cirrus network. (See Appendix D, "PDA Software to Go: Download Resources," for more on helpful web clipping applications for the traveler.)

Bet You Didn't Know

Encrypting data on a PDA might seem like overkill, but if you require serious security, you might want to take advantage of the several programs that can scramble your data, so it only makes sense to you. Moviancrypt encrypts all the data on a PDA so that it is unintelligible to someone who doesn't have the correct password. The software works on Palm OS 3.0 and later and Windows CE. You can purchase the software at moviansecurity.com for $39.95.

The encryption process is sophisticated and clever; data is scrambled based on a mathematical formula using your password and a line you scribble on the PDA's screen. The password and scribble get translated into numbers. When these two numbers are plugged into the formula, your encryption key is created.

Insurance for PDA

Invariably, something can always go wrong with your PDA that might or might not be your fault. A drop from a desk? It could happen to anybody. A little coffee in the serial port? Happens all the time.

You can insure laptops and PDAs for a relatively small amount of money (especially considering that some new PDAs cost as much as laptops, between $500 and nearly $1,000 for a Handheld PC, with keyboard, from Hewlett Packard).

Safeware (www.safeware.com) provides insurance for fire, theft, and yes, just about whatever you spill in the keyboard. Tornado? Covered. Earthquake? Yep. They do not, however, cover nuclear disaster. So you're on your own in that case.

Mobile phones, including smart phones, typically offer insurance from the service provider at a small monthly fee. If you leave your phone behind somewhere on a trip, you'll thank yourself for getting the insurance.

Synch Phone for Rainy Day

It can be a real hassle synching up more than one device, especially if you enter information on your desktop at work and enter information into your phone and PDA on the road. You can synch everything at once, though, if you're willing to pay extra to do so.

Using software and a serial cable, you can synch your smart phone's contact names and numbers to your PC's personal organizer software, and then synch your PDA. FoneSync PRO makes it easy to back up all your contact information and make sure it's current on all your devices. The kit, which includes a software and cable, costs about $80, at www.fonesynch.com. You need to check (online) to see if the software works with your phone model.

Making Sure You Have Power

Getting a strong signal on your wireless modem is a lot easier if you have power. But batteries can go dead at the most inconvenient times. Also, your power adapter can go bad just when you need it. If you have the bucks, and you want to be sure you'll have power, check out the Universal AC Adapter from Targus (www.targus.com), shown in Figure 20.3.

Figure 20.3

An eight-tip universal power adapter for laptops. More tips are available from Targus for PDAs.

The adapter is lightweight (less than eight ounces) and comes with eight power tips that fit into the adapter ports of most laptops. You can also buy other tips for other devices. It works on PDAs, laptops, and phones. It's expensive, but potentially worth the price to cover every device you carry, at $120. (Extra tips cost $20 each, yikes.)

If you're traveling by train, note that an increasing number of Amtrak train cars are equipped with a 120-volt outlet at every seat. Even older models without the seatside AC have a couple of concealed outlets that the conductor will help you find. You could switch seats to use them or bring a really long extension, if the present occupant isn't cooperative.

Keep Yourself Free of Spam

On a handheld over a pokey wireless connection, who wants to be weighed down with spam? The best way to cut down on junk mail is to keep your main e-mail address a secret.

Here's how: Set up a free e-mail account at Hotmail, Netscape, or your free Web-based e-mail provider of choice. Give out your new, just-for-spam, address when asked (such as when you're shopping online) for a valid e-mail address. If you really need to, you can check the address later for legitimate mail. In fact, it's a good idea to scan past all the spam every couple weeks or so to make sure there's not an e-mail there you need to read. Then just trash all the junk.

Keep your main e-mail address from appearing in public places, such as online bulletin boards, newsgroups, and Web pages. And never reply to junk e-mail, even if it gives instructions on how to be removed from the list. A reply is often just a confirmation to the spammer that the address is connected to a real person.

If you check your main e-mail account on your wireless devices, you're probably already suffering from spam. Many Internet service providers offer smart software on their server (so you don't have to mess with it) that can really help you cut down on junk mail and get more done on your wireless device. Check with your ISP about its spam controls, and use them.

The Least You Need to Know

- ◆ You can protect yourself, and recover, from electrical surges, snapped antennas, and other road hazards with a few inexpensive PDA, laptop, and smart phone add-ons.

- ◆ Wireless Internet in the sky? Major airline carriers are working with Boeing to provide wireless broadband Internet access by satellite in the air.

- ◆ You can protect PDA data by encrypting it, should it fall into the wrong hands.

- ◆ Another way to protect your PDA is to insure it. You can pay to cover your laptops and PDAs in case of accidental damage. Most wireless phone providers offer insurance for lost and damaged phones.

- ◆ Free yourself from spam on your wireless devices by carefully protecting your e-mail address. Find out if your Internet service provider uses spam controls, and enable them.

Optimizing Wireless Computing

In This Chapter

- ◆ Saving battery power
- ◆ Faster wireless browsing
- ◆ Adding tools for faster text input
- ◆ Speeding up wireless home and office networks

Although we laud wireless technology for the mobility and freedom it provides, to be honest, there are areas where it could use some improvement. In this chapter we'll look at ways to make wireless technology faster, last longer, and act more reliably.

Making wireless devices work more efficiently sometimes means adding a feature or tool. Other times it means reducing things you don't need, such as blinking Web banners.

It's clear that the world is moving toward wireless computing. With the tips in this chapter, you'll be able to make sure you stay connected smartly, even when you unplug.

Saving Batteries on Your PDA

A dead battery can put the kibosh on your wireless plans. Extending battery life is important when you're wireless, and you can do so in a handful of ways.

First, if your PDA uses a color screen, consider reducing the brightness (see Figure 21.1). Even using a slightly less luminous screen, can result in a noticeable extension of your battery life. And of course, backlighting (which helps you see your PDAs screen in the dark) eats up power, so use it sparingly when battery life is low. It's a good idea to carry a couple of extra AAA batteries around for your Palm or Handspring device and most stores carry them.

Figure 21.1

Reducing brightness on a Palm-OS handheld.

If you're a Palm user, turn off Beaming. You can turn it on again by pressing the **Address Book** button, which has a phone icon on it, for two seconds (signaling that you're ready to beam a business card) and then you're asked if you want to turn on the Beaming feature again.

Speeding Up Your Wireless Network

Want to eek out more performance from your wireless network? Turn off encryption for a speed boost. If you don't feel that your data needs the security of encryption, turn it off (see Figure 21.2).

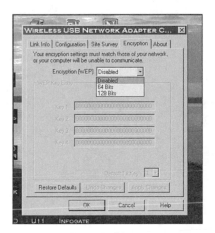

Figure 21.2

Turning off encryption over a wireless network.

Encryption takes processing power, which can reduce the speed of your access point. If you're in a situation, say at home, where wireless encryption isn't an issue, just disable it at your individual computers and at the access point (if you have one).

Turning Off Graphics When Browsing

If you use a wireless modem or a Webphone connected to your laptop, a great way to get more speed when you browse is to turn off graphics in your browser (see Figure 21.3).

True, some sites aren't set up for picture-free browsing. But most are. When I travel and connect through my mobile phone, my laptop is almost always set up to browse graphic-free. You'll be surprised how well it can work.

Figure 21.3

Say good-bye to slow-loading graphics, and say hello to speedy wireless Web surfing.

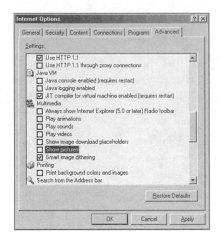

Watch Out!

You might be downloading more data than you need. Reducing the amount of data you download is the first step in speeding up your surfing. Web browsers typically offer the option to turn off images in the Preferences or Options menu. Doing so dramatically improves your ability to move around the Web. PDAs and smart phones typically reduce the amount of graphics you see, by design, so this is less of a worry with handheld wireless devices.

Getting a Stowable Keyboard

Optimizing wireless computing isn't just about taking a Spartan approach. Sometimes you need to add a little something, like a portable keyboard for your PDA or phone.

It's hard to type e-mail and edit word processing documents without a keyboard. (I'm not talking about the tiny keyboard menu that displays on your PDA screen.)

Keyboards run about $70 to $100, and you can find them at many local electronics stores and online sellers, including iGO.com and PalmGear.com.

The Motorola iBoard Keyboard from Think Outside fits in the palm of your hand (see Figure 21.4). Fully extended, it connects to Motorola i85s and i50sx wireless handsets.

Figure 21.4

The Motorola iBoard Keyboard from Think Outside.

(Photo courtesy of Think Outside)

The Stowaway Keyboard by Think Outside (see Figure 21.5) works with a range of PDAs, including Palm, Handspring, HP Jornada, Compaq iPAQ, or Sony CLIE.

Figure 21.5

The Stowaway Keyboard by Think Outside.

(Photo courtesy of Think Outside)

Bet You Didn't Know

The T9 feature found on many Web phones enables you to enter text by pressing just one key per letter. The technology recognizes common words from certain key combinations and prompts you to choose the one you want (or the next most commonly used word using the key sequence you typed). To enter the word "how," for example, you press the keys 4, 6, and 9. The multi-tap method used by other phones requires that you press one key multiple times to choose a single letter. Note that T9 must be embedded in the phone—you can't add it on later. When selecting a phone, you may want to consider whether T9 is included. Note that T9 technology is owned by America Online.

Downloading a Web-Clipping App

Palm users who need to surf quickly should consider Web-clipping applications (sometimes called *PQAs*), which are small programs for the Palm OS.

The Palm VII and VIIx have a built-in wireless modem and are ready to use PQAs out of the box (you will need to purchase a wireless modem or connect a Palm handheld to a mobile phone using a cable to use Web-clipping applications with other Palm handhelds). Web clipping applications make a request to an Internet site without showing you all the elements of the site, so that you can quickly get to the information you need.

Sure, you can download (www.download.com) an HTML Web browser, and see graphics and blinking ads—the whole shebang. But, if you just want the information you need, and want it quickly, try a Web-clipping application. Download a PQA, follow the instructions that come with it, and the next time you synch up, the PQA will be ready to use on your Palm handheld (see Figure 21.6).

Well-Connected Words

Palm Web-clipping applications are also called **PQAs** (Palm Query Applications). These little programs enable you to quickly send requests to search engines, shopping sites, travel planners—about 400 sites—that cover just about anything that you'd prefer to browse graphic-free when on the Web. Some Palm OS handhelds, including Visors, require that you install a Web-clipping browser to view the .pqa files.

Figure 21.6

Downloading a Web-clipping application from PalmGear.com.

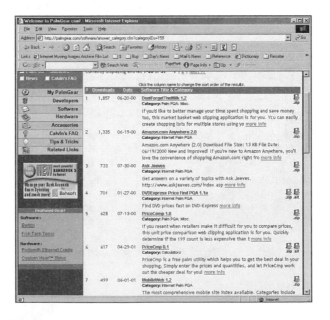

Because most PDA browsers don't let you download files or use cookies, browsing by PDA results in a limited Web experience no matter how you go online. (There just isn't enough memory on many PDAs for handling downloaded files.) Save yourself some more time by using a PQA, and cut down on some of the Web "noise," including animated ads.

Web Phone: Make Bookmarks

If you use a smart phone to browse the Internet, you probably aren't using the bookmark feature as much as you could be. (I know I'm guilty of this and pay for it when I need to press keys more often than necessary to reach a site and log in.)

Every smart phone offers a bookmarking feature. This feature enables you to assign a bookmarked Internet site to a key on the phone's keypad, for even faster browsing. Most carriers (such as Sprint PCS, VoiceStream, and ALLTEL) enable you to choose the bookmarks you see and in what order, by logging on to their Web sites and setting your preferences. The changes you make on the Web site then appear on your phone.

Most smart phones allow you to press a key on the phone to bookmark the page you're viewing, for faster retrieval later (see Figure 21.7). In this example, you would press the 9 key to view a list of the sites you often visit.

Figure 21.7

Press a key on the phone to bookmark the page you're viewing, for faster retrieval later.

(Photo courtesy of My Docs Online, Inc.)

Using a Web Phone Accelerator

You can use a Web accelerator for the times you connect your Web phone to your laptop. Sprint PCS, for instance, ships a Web accelerator, called Blue Kite, with its wireless Web connectivity kit. You install the program along with the dialing software for the Web phone. OmniSky, Sprint PCS, and Sierra Wireless use Blue Kite.

The accelerator compresses text and images that are downloaded to your PDA, reducing the amount of data that is sent, which should give the impression of a faster connection.

Adding a New Modem to Your Old Account

A tip for the frugal optimizer with an eye for consolidation: If you're considering purchasing a wireless modem, see if you can add it to your existing calling plan.

If you need to purchase yet another calling plan to use a wireless modem, you'll be billed simply for the privilege of access. Some wireless providers allow you to bundle the modem onto your existing plan, saving you some cash in the process.

The Least You Need to Know

- You can save battery power on your PDA or laptop by unplugging your modem when you don't need it, reducing the brightness of a color screen, and turning off Beaming.

- Turning off the encryption on a wireless network can boost speed, which is great for those times you are not worried about the security of transmitting your network's data wirelessly.

- T9 technology and add-on keyboards can make smart phones and PDAs more useful, respectively, when entering text on wireless handheld devices.

- ◆ You can use Web-clipping, graphics-free browsing, and software browsing accelerators to speed up your Web-surfing experience.

- ◆ Smart phone bookmarks and accelerators are two ways to save time when surfing the wireless Internet.

- ◆ Looking to save a buck? Try adding a wireless modem to your existing mobile phone account, potentially avoiding unnecessary charges.

Chapter 22

Future Tech

In This Chapter

- G thing: third generation broadband
- Smarter phones and PDAs
- Near future, short range: Bluetooth
- Super speedy wireless networks

When you spend your hard-earned cash on electronics, you might sometimes get the feeling that they will be obsolete the second the automatic door closes behind you at the store. To some degree, that can't be helped.

On the upside, future technologies, especially in wireless computing, are being introduced at a rapid pace and are driving up the speed of computing and driving down price. On the downside, that speedy pace frequently means new technologies are often incompatible with the existing ones you're using.

In this chapter we'll look at what's coming around in the near future—sorry, no jetpack stuff here. You won't find how to make an Internet connection from the space shuttle or launch your own satellite, but you will find out about what's around the corner. If you're window-shopping now, there might be some products for which waiting will be both virtuous and profitable.

G Thing: Third Generation Wireless

Faster Internet surfing is always in demand; and right now, cellular networks aren't really speedy enough to make the surfing experience much fun. In the near future, Wireless service providers will offer something that handles voice calling, and wireless Internet access at broadband speed, through 3G (the third generation of mobile cellular communications).

Since we've moved from 1G (analog technology) to 2G (digital technology), it's become easier to surf the Internet by phone—or use your phone as a modem. Until now, wireless technology was designed for voice, so the first two generations of wireless service are comparatively slow for transmitting data, allowing the transfer of 7 to 19kbps. Now, in the United States, we're starting to see 2.5G, faster mobile cellular networks capable of broadband speeds. GPRS, for example, is a 2.5 technology, which can move data at 144kbps. AT&T Wireless, Cingular, and VoiceStream are planning to offer the wireless standard. Sprint PCS and Verizon are backing a competing 2.5 technology, an upgrade to the CDMA standard that will offer similar speeds.

What wireless enthusiasts really get excited about, though, is 3G, which promises speeds that can accommodate more multimedia-friendly applications, such as video and streaming audio—just about anything you can get on the Web—on your phone or PDA. 3G could also be useful for connecting laptops to phones that dial in to office networks, for fast access to data when workers are out of the office.

At maximum, 3G is predicted to transfer data at rates of between 64kbps and 2mbps (now that's fast). The possibilities are wide open, from sharing pictures of your kids over your phone to watching movies on your PDA. Unfortunately, the devices and the networks won't be up to speed for a few more years, with target dates for widespread distribution hovering around 2004.

Just when you get up to speed on 3G, 4G (fourth generation wireless) starts nosing around to confuse you. 3G concerns itself with the ability to more speedily and efficiently handle voice calls and Internet access; 4G aims to make wireless networks more compatible.

Currently, you're faced with an alphabet soup of networks that probably mean little to you, such as CDMA, TDMA, GSM, and others. The aim of 4G is to get wireless phone networks, Bluetooth devices (see Figure 21.1), and even satellite Internet access working together so that working wirelessly on the Internet is less of a hassle.

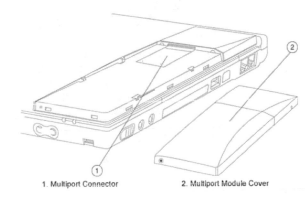

Figure 22.1

A Bluetooth add-on device for a Compaq notebook.

(Photo courtesy of Compaq Computer Corporation)

1. Multiport Connector   2. Multiport Module Cover

Smarter Phones and PDAs

The integration of personal organizer software and smart phones is becoming more common. As phones mature into more advanced organizers, expect to see versions of the Palm and Windows CE operating system on their tiny screens—Microsoft's *Stinger* OS is a good example (see Figure 22.2).

Some smart phones and PDAs run the EPOC operating system from Symbian, which offers personal information management features. Symbian is jointly owned by Psion, Motorola, Nokia, Ericsson (see Figure 22.3), and Panasonic. Smart phones that use the Symbian operating system include the Ericsson R380 and the Nokia 9210/9290.

Figure 22.2

Mitsubishi's Trium Mondo offers personal organizer software, the Mobile Explorer browser, and the Pocket PC operating system also known as Stinger. The phone will be sold in Europe and might be sold later in the United States.

Well-Connected Words

Microsoft's mini version of Windows CE for smart phones, currently called **Stinger,** looks similar to what you find on Pocket PC handhelds. The phones provide many organizer features, such as an address book and reminder alarms, and they synch up to the data on your PC.

What do smarter phones mean for you? Well, you'll likely have an easier time synching your phone with your e-mail program, because these are mature technologies that have been handling the job for years.

More important, it could mean leaving an extra device at home. Taking a phone, a laptop, and a PDA is overkill if one device can take care of the job. Being mobile doesn't mean taking everything that beeps along with you for the ride. You can take a phone with PDA features, or a PDA with phone features—whatever suits you.

Figure 22.3

The Ericsson R380 is a smart phone that runs the Symbian EPOC operating system and offers PDA-like features, such as contact lists, e-mail, calendar, and a WAP browser.

Near Future, Short Range: Bluetooth

The future of Bluetooth, a very promising wireless networking technology that automatically connects all sorts of electronics within range of each other (up to 30 feet), is still unclear.

Many technology watchers thought we would be using Bluetooth enabled PDAs, notebooks, cell phones, and other electronics extensively by now. The technology is handy at connecting multiple devices wirelessly so that, for instance, a room of smart phones and PDAs can trade information. Vendors are working on Bluetooth camcorders that could enable you to connect your camera wirelessly to your television for watching home movies.

In the future, you might, have a tiny wireless headset that connects to a cell phone on your belt. An e-mail sent from a PDA could use the cell phone's radio module. When you get in your car, the headset could connect you to your car phone, and your PDA would act as the display screen for your GPS, offering maps and directions as you drive. All the devices could share information wirelessly using Bluetooth.

Currently though, not many devices support Bluetooth. For the technology to take off, more electronics will need to communicate by Bluetooth so that consumers come to rely on the technology.

Home Networking Speedups

As it stands, you have several choices if you want to set up a wireless network at your home or office: 802.11b (Wi-Fi) and, to a lesser extent, HomeRF. Things could get more complicated as both technologies move toward faster transmission speeds.

Synch Up

Wireless networking should get a boost out of 802.11a, a soon-to-be standard that will push data at a theoretical maximum speed of 54mbps. In a word: zoom! If you're currently considering 802.11b, which has a maximum transfer rate of 11mbps, seriously think about waiting for 802.11a equipment to hit the shelves and get more bang for your buck.

Although few vendors make HomeRF products these days, the ones that do are going to start making devices that jump from transfer rates of 1.6mpbs to transfer rates of 10mbps, in the second version of the standard. The updated version of the technology might be available by the time you read this. That could be a meaningful improvement, because HomeRF products are focused on the ability to handle telephone voice service and multimedia over their wireless networks. A later version of HomeRF is planned to blaze along at 54mbps, so there's still some kick to this technology.

At the same time, Wi-Fi is also looking to gain momentum, pushing for faster speeds and better multimedia support. Its wide support in airports and hotels continues to expand, and some ISPs might even be able to offer you wireless, and inexpensive, 802.11b service with quick install times, right in your home. The ability to use wireless broadband at home, and for travel, is very promising.

Satellite Internet Advances

Currently, Internet speeds for those who connect by satellite are limited to about 500kbps downloading and about 140kbps uploading. Speeds in the near future are expected to move at 1.5mbps and, potentially, much faster.

Low-earth-orbit satellites (LEO) have the potential to give a boost to satellite broadband (see Figure 22.4). LEOs orbit 200 to 400 miles above the Earth as opposed to 22,300 miles, such as the satellites that currently provide two-way satellite Internet access (DirecWay and Starband). Because the data has less distance to travel to a LEO, it moves from sender to receiver faster, removing irksome delays that plague real-time applications like video teleconferencing. The trouble is, you need a constellation of hundreds of these LEO satellites to move your data across the world, and such a fleet is extremely expensive to launch.

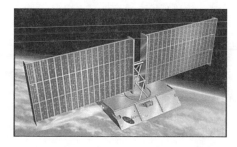

Figure 22.4

A Teledesic low-earth-orbit satellite (LEO).

(Photo courtesy of Teledesic)

Teledesic is the leading developer of LEO satellites and has a widely publicized investor in Microsoft Chairman Bill Gates, among other financial celebrities. The service was initially planned to launch in 2001 but has seen a series of delays and isn't expected to start until 2005.

The Least You Need to Know

- ◆ As we look into our crystal ball, 3G appears, ambling toward Internet users who want to hit the road with fast network speeds for smart phones that can handle multimedia, including music and (small) videos.

- ◆ As we speak, more phones and PDAs are being combined, so you can carry around one smarter device for voice, editing documents, and Internet access.

- ◆ Wireless home and office networking, growing in popularity, will reach faster speeds and deliver multimedia more reliably in the near future.

- ◆ Fast Internet service by satellite is available now, but even faster service, provided by low-earth-orbiting satellites, is on the way.

Glossary: Speak Like a Geek

1G This refers to the first generation of analog cellular technology.

2G In the 1990s, digital second generation phones were introduced, used primarily for voice and text messaging.

3G We should see third generation, or 3G, phones in the next few years. The technology will provide faster transmission and global roaming capability. We may also use 3G technologies for high-quality, wireless audio and video transmission.

802.11 A group of wireless standards that lets you connect computers to a network for sharing files and Internet connections.

802.11b Sometimes called Wi-Fi, this is a wireless standard that enables you to connect computers to a network. You can find 802.11b devices at most electronics or computer stores. The standard makes it easy to set up a network that you can use to share files and printers between computers, or share an Internet connection. 802.11b transfers data at a maximum rate of 11mbps. 802.11a transfers data at a maximum speed of 54mbps.

access point This wireless networking device lets you tie a wireless network into a wired network. An access point communicates with the wireless networking cards you install in each computer in a network.

ad hoc   In this wireless network setup, each computer you want to connect to the network needs a wireless networking card. The computers will connect directly to each other. In an *infrastructure* network, by contrast, wireless network cards all communicate with a central *access point*.

AMPS (Advanced Mobile Phone Stytem)   The analog cell phone standard.

beam   To send information from one device (such as a PDA) to another wirelessly, using infrared light.

bit (binary digit)   This is the smallest amount of data a computer can store, a 0 or a 1. It takes eight bits to make a byte, which represents a letter, number, or symbol.

BlackBerry handheld   A wireless paging device from Research In Motion (RIM). BlackBerry handhelds and pager-sized devices send and receive e-mails and have limited Internet browsing capability. You can also use a BlackBerry to send a fax or access Microsoft Outlook or Lotus Notes servers.

Bluetooth   A fast (720kbps) method of transferring data short distances from mobile devices, such as laptops and PDAs, to desktop computers.

broadband   Network access operating at speeds meeting or exceeding those of fast-wired technologies such as DSL and cable modems. Broadband is often used in reference to Internet access.

CDPD (Cellular Digital Packet Data)   This is a digital wireless network used to transmit data at a maximum rate of 19.2kbps. Most wireless modems use CDPD to connect to the Internet.

cellular   Mobile phones are sometimes called cellular, or cell phones, because the geographic area in which they can send and receive a signal is called a cell. Many cells make up a coverage area.

CompactFlash   A socket built into some PDAs (such as many Pocket PCs) can be used to connect PDAs to wireless modems, mobile phones, and local network adapters (see www.socketcom.com). The CompactFlash card, connected to a cable, slides into a CompactFlash socket on your PDA. CompactFlash cards are often used with PDAs and other small electronics, such as digital cameras, for removable storage. A CompactFlash card is about one-third the size of a PC Card.

cradle   This is a type of docking station used to connect a handheld device to a computer for downloading Web pages, programs, e-mail, and updating contact lists and calendars, as well as other data between a computer and PDA or smart phone.

encryption   A process that converts data into a scrambled code so that it cannot easily be intercepted without authorization.

EPOC   An operating system from Symbian used in PDAs and mobile phones.

Ethernet   The most common type of wired network. The technology can reach a maximum data transfer speed of 100mbps and is used to share computers, printers, and Internet connections.

GPRS (General Packet Radio Service)   This is a digital cellular phone standard, an update to GSM networks, that can send and receive data at a speed between 56kbps and 114kbps.

GPS (global positioning system)   This is system of 24 satellites, which was launched by the U.S. Department of Defense. A handheld GPS receiver can triangulate signals from three or more satellites and provide your location— including altitude—anywhere in the world.

GSM (Global System for Mobile Communications)   Used by most of the rest of the world outside the United States, GSM (PCS 1900) is the digital cellular standard in Europe.

HomeRF   This wireless local area network (LAN) standard transfers data at 1.6mbps. Like 802.11b and OpenAir, HomeRF equipment transmits in the 2.4GHz range. HomeRF is often cited for its ability to broadcast both voice and data.

infrared   A beam of light that requires a clear line of site for transmission of data, such as a document sent from one PDA or laptop to another. Many PDAs and laptops use the IrDA (Infrared Data Association) standard for infrared transmission. Note that the Palm OS does not use IrDA.

infrastructure   In this wireless network configuration, all your wireless access cards communicate with an access point, in contrast to an ad hoc wireless network.

IrDA   Many PDAs and laptops use the IrDA (Infrared Data Association) standard for infrared transmission between computers, phones, and PDAs.

LAN (local area network)   A group of connected computers. A wireless, or wired, LAN allows you to share data, including Internet access, among all connected computers.

latency   In reference to satellite Internet access, the delay in the time between when you click a link while surfing the Web on your computer and when you receive a Web page, by way of a satellite 22,300 miles above.

OpenAir   This wireless networking technology, like HomeRF, transfers data at 1.6mbps and operates in the 2.4GHz band.

Palm OS   The operating system used by Palm handhelds.

PC Card expansion slot   Sometimes called PCMCIA; enables you to add peripherals to your laptop, such as wireless modems, networking cards, and nonwireless gear like removable storage and memory.

PCS (Personal Communications Services)   This is a term that refers to both voice and data services, such as voicemail, caller ID, and wireless Internet access, communicating in the 1,900MHz band.

PDA (Personal Digital Assistant)   A handheld device used to manage e-mail, contacts, appointments, and, if connected to a wireless modem, access the Internet.

Pocket PC   This is Microsoft's name for handheld computers that run the Pocket PC operating system (or the OS formerly known as Windows CE, version 3.0). The devices typically come with a stylus and compete with the Palm OS handhelds.

PQA (Palm Query Application)   If you use a Palm device to access the Internet, you may need to download a Web-clipping application (called a PQA, or Palm Query App) to access the information from some sites.

QWERTY   A keyboard that takes its name from the top-left six keys of most keyboards. Invented in 1868 by Christopher Sholes, who also invented the typewriter, the QWERTY keyboard is still the most popular in use. Some say the configuration of letters was created to slow down fast typists and keep the keys from jamming. Others say this slow-moving story behind the design of the keyboard is just a myth.

roaming   Occurs when you travel outside your provider's wireless network. Sometimes roaming occurs when you are outside a digital calling network and use an analog one. A phone that can use both digital and analog networks is often called a dual-mode phone. Here's the catch: The charges associated with roaming are pretty confusing, so make sure you understand how you'll be billed when you sing up for a plan. In some cases there may be charge for voice roaming, but not for data roaming. Definitions of roaming can vary widely—be prepared.

router   Enables you to connect two networks. You can use a router to give multiple computers the capability to share a single Internet connection. For example, to set up your computers to share a DSL modem, you can plug a router into one port in a hub, plug a modem in the other port, and plug your computers in the rest of the available ports.

smart phone   This is a generic name for a mobile phone that can send and receive e-mail and instant messages, and browse the Internet, typically using a WAP browser.

SMS (Short Messaging System)   This is a means of sending short messages, usually no more than 160 characters, using a mobile phone.

standard   This is a specification that vendors agree to for the development of a product. Standards often help products from different manufacturers work together.

Stinger   Microsoft's mini version of Windows CE for smart phones; looks similar to what you find on Pocket PC handhelds. The phones provide many organizer features, such as an address book and reminder alarms, and they synch up to the data on your PC.

streaming   Allows you to watch or listen to multimedia as it downloads to your computer (instead of waiting for the entire file to download, and then viewing). Wireless networks are handy for using streaming multimedia, since you can check out audio and video from another computer on your network anywhere in your house. You can take your laptop out by the pool and watch a video on the hard drive of your PC upstairs.

switch   Connects computers together in a traditional, wired Ethernet network. A switch can also be used to create a subnetwork, so that the computers plugged into it don't affect the larger network traffic. You can connect a switch as a standalone element of your network, or your access point might have a switch built in.

T9   A feature found on many Web phones that lets you enter text by pressing just one key per letter. The technology recognizes common words from certain key combinations and prompts you to choose the one you want (or the next most commonly used word using the key sequence you typed). To enter the word "how," for example, you type the keys 4, 6, and 9.

WAN (wide area network)   A wireless WAN can provide network (primarily Internet) access over a large geographic region.

WAP (Wireless Application Protocol)   A standard that lets developers create applications that can be viewed using a browser on a Web phone or PDA.

Web clipping   A way of displaying information from the Web on the small screen of a phone or PDA. The Palm OS devices use Web clipping to speed up retrieval of information from the Internet over wireless connections, while leaving behind images to save time.

Web phone   *See* smart phone.

Web portal   This is a site on the Internet that aggregates all sorts of content into one place. You typically find free e-mail accounts, news, sports, entertainment, stocks, and other information you would usually search for all over the Web.

WEP (Wired Equivalent Privacy)   A method of encrypting data over a wireless 802.11b network. This protocol is meant to protect wireless LANs (local area networks), which are inherently more vulnerable to unauthorized access since the network data is transferred over radio waves.

wireless narrowband   In contrast to fast-moving wireless broadband, is the name for the monochrome, small-screen Internet access we currently see in mobile phones and two-way pagers. Typically these devices connect at 9.6kbps to 14.4kbps.

WML (Wireless Markup Language)   The language used by Web designers to construct pages, called cards, for wireless devices. The language is similar to HTML (Hypertext Markup Language), which is the coding used to construct World Wide Web pages. If you've ever worked with your own Web pages, you probably can pick up WML pretty easily. Check out Builder.com (www.builder.com) for more information on creating your own WML pages.

workgroup   In Microsoft networking, a workgroup is a collection of computers on your network that all go by the same name.

Outlets Ahoy

Although a book on wireless computing is bound to be partial to cordless technology, it should be pointed out that you probably already have the makings of a network in your home or office, using existing wiring.

Phone-line and power-line networks, while not as flexible, offer some of the same benefits of wireless networks, because they reduce the number of wires needed to connect your computers. Phone-line networks, in particular, are relatively inexpensive and simple to set up, and you don't have wires running all over the place (or have to drop cables and install face plates in the wall).

There are, of course, downsides to these technologies. They don't work in every home, and you might not found out they don't work until you try them. Yet before you invest in a wireless network, it's not a bad idea to know about other options that are available at your local electronics store or online computer shop.

Phone-Line Networks

Phone-line networks are, like wireless networks, relatively inexpensive, easy to install, and fast. Wherever you have a phone connection, you can plug into the network and trade files, surf the Internet, or play MP3 audio files.

HomePNA (Home Phoneline Network Alliance) is a phone-line network that uses common phone wiring (also called RJ-11), which simplifies setting up a home or small-office network. HomePNA comes in two flavors. An earlier version of the technology, which came out in 1998, offered a maximum speed of 1mbps. The 2.0 specification, which is currently available, is compatible with the earlier technology and provides a maximum bandwidth of 10mpbs.

You can purchase a kit that includes everything you need to create a home network. To get started, you plug a phone-line adapter card into a computer's PCI slot and attach a phone cord from the card to the phone jack.

Some phone-line kits offer a USB connection rather than a PCI card, enabling you to get started by plugging a cable into a USB-equipped computer rather than opening the case to install a PCI card, which might appeal to those who aren't comfortable with the innards of their PCs.

The first iteration of phone-line networks was slow (about 1mbps), but the second version of the phone-line networks (called the HomePNA 2.0 specification) runs at 10mbps. That's close to the maximum speeds of a Wi-Fi network, and is fast enough for surfing the Web.

Of course, you're still tied to rooms with wall jacks or areas where you don't mind exposed phone cords. Wireless local area networks obviously have the edge here. And in about 20 percent of homes (especially in older homes), due to wiring incompatibilities, products based on the HomePNA 2.0 specification don't work. The older, 1.0 specification, which runs at 1mbps, works in all but about 1 percent of homes.

Connecting with Existing House Wiring

Using your house wiring is another relatively inexpensive way to connect your computers. You probably have plenty of outlets, and considering ease of setup, power-line networks are considered by some analysts to be the most likely home networking product to really take off.

Power-line networking has been around for some time, but products have only recently settled on a standard, so the new devices, often called Home-Plug, are just getting started.

Early power-line products drew the ire of consumers who found the products too slow and unreliable. The new specification calls for products with a maximum bandwidth of 14mbps, which makes them slightly faster than the other commonly used home and small-office networking products.

Like Wi-Fi devices, power-line networks are fast enough for browsing the Internet, yet not as fast as the speediest Ethernet devices, which offer a maximum data transfer rate of 100mpbs.

Wireless networking still appears to be a better bet than power-line products, primarily because the current wireless standards have been on the market longer and have proven to be simple to set up and use. Power-line technology might yet turn out to be the technology that makes home networking take off, but as of this writing, it's too early to tell.

For now, wireless is the speed and ease-of-setup technology to beat. The following is a breakdown of some wired and wireless home networks:

♦ **Technology:** Phone-line

How it works: Insert a network card into computer. Plug standard (RJ 11) phone cable into the adapter and plug the other end into a wall jack.

Maximum bandwidth: 10mpbs

Pro: Lots of products available. Easy to set up.

Con: You may not have a phone jack near your computer.

♦ **Technology:** Power-line

How it works: Install network cards in each PC you want to use. Connect cards to electrical outlet.

Maximum bandwidth: 14mbps

Pro: Plugs into any electrical outlet in your home or office.

Con: These products are just getting off the ground, so there hasn't been a lot of testing on reliability and data rates.

◆ **Technology:** Wireless (802.11b)

How it works: Insert a card, which acts like a radio transmitter into each computer you plan to network.

Maximum bandwidth: 11mbps

Pro: Easiest technology to set up. Works through walls. No other technology gives you as much freedom to work from wherever you want.

Con: Distance limited by obstructions. More expensive than other home-networking technologies.

WAP Directory: Sites Worth Checking Out

Most smart phones come with a handful of WAP sites featured in the display. Here are some suggestions for WAP sites you might want to bookmark yourself.

First Stop: Portals

AOL, MSN, and Yahoo! offer mobile sites where you can check your e-mail or online calendar, plus news, finance, and weather.

AOL

Web/WAP site: www.myaol.com

Yahoo!

Web site: www.yahoo.com

WAP site: wap.yahoo.com

MSN

Web site: www.msn.com

WAP site: mobile.msn.com

WAP Info, Anyone?

Gelon.net   Gelon.net has one of the most unusual design interfaces you're likely to find. The site allows you to view WAP sites using an emulator that looks like a collection of popular WAP phones. Fun and easy to use.

Web site: www.gelon.net

WAP site: wap.gelon.net

Cellmania   This extensive site reviews and ranks WAP sites. Even more handy, the site provides a WAP emulator so you can "test drive" each site reviewed. If you just bought a WAP phone, this should be one of your first stops.

Web site: www.cellmania.com

WAP site: wap.cellmania.com

Wap.com   Offers a directory of WAP sites, phone and PDA reviews, plus news. A recent headline: "Mobile phones and PDAs can replace hotel keys and remote controls in the nearest future." Neat. Includes a WAP emulator.

Web site: www.wap.com

WAP site: wap.com

Finding Your Way on the Go

Hollywood.com   The service is a fast way to get the latest movie listings and offers news, show times, reviews, and entertainment gossip. The service even offers directions to the nearest theater.

Web site: www.hollywood.com

WAP site: wap.hollywood.com

MapQuest   MapQuest offers turn-by-turn driving directions. The service is very helpful if you know the address of your destination.

Web site: www.mapquest.com

WAP site: wireless.mapquest.com/attws/suite

myW@Ptrans   This handy WAP site allows you to translate words from English, German, French, Turkish, Danish, Spanish, Japanese, Russian, and Italian. *Meraviglioso!* (Wonderful!)

Web site: www.hazar.com/dictionary.html

WAP site: www.hazar.com/dictionary.wml

WhereEverYouGo   Type in your current location and within seconds you'll have a list of restaurants, bars, pharmacies, groceries, gas stations, and other businesses in your area. The service provides the address, phone number, distance, and direction of the business from where you are.

Web site: www.everywhereyougo.com

WAP site: www.weyg.com

Extra, Extra: News, Sports, and Weather

123 Jump   Need financial news on the go? This WAP service offers stock quotes, market information, financial glossary, and news and analysis. You'll know about the most active stocks of the day before you get off the train home from work.

WAP/Web site: www.123jump.com

Financial Times   A scaled-down version of the FT.com Web site, the WAP FT offers excellent national, international, and market news. You can find the top stories of the day, read through business briefs, or check a stock quote.

Web site: www.ft.com

WAP site: wap.ft.com

The Weather Channel   This familiar name provides cloud conditions, humidity, wind speed, and temperature, barometer readings, and five-day weather forecasts for cities in the USA.

Web site: www.weather.com

WAP site: wireless.weather.com/wireless/att/index.hdml

CBS Sports Online   Offers updated scores, news, and fantasy scoring on major sports in the country.

WAP/Web site: cbs.sportline.com

ESPN.com   Provides news, scores, standings, and rankings of the major professional leagues and college sports. I spent half an hour reading an ESPN The Magazine story in the DMV once. You can bet I've bookmarked it since.

Web site: www.espn.com

WAP site: wap.espn.com

Reference: Call Somebody's Bet

LookWAYUp   A simple dictionary for finding meanings in a pinch.

Web site: www.lookwayup.com

WAP site: wap.lookwayup.com

PhonaFact   You're in a business meeting when somebody makes a claim that's hard to back up. No problem. Check out searchable reference portal offering dictionary/thesaurus and sports, geography, history, plus a conversion tool for currencies, volume, area, length, and temperature. Don't be fooled again.

WAP/Web site: www.phoneafact.com

Shopping: Dial Up a Deal

Barpoint.com   A number of sites use numeric product identifiers to find and compare products. Barpoint.com enables you to type in a product's bar code (or a book's ISBN). You can also search by product name.

WAP/Web site: www.barpoint.com

Pricegrabber.com   Pricegrabber.com is a comparison-shopping site with a numeric twist. You can enter a model number or part number of product you're bargain-hunting for. If you don't know the part or model number, you can browse by category or search by keyword.

Web site: www.pricegrabber.com

WAP site: atpgw.com

mySimon   One of the most comprehensive shopping sites around, mySimon lists product information and pricing from 2,000 online stores, including computers, clothes, flowers, and sporting goods. When you're ready to buy, click a link, and you'll arrive at the merchant's site.

Web site: www.mysimon.com

WAP site: wap.mysimon.com

PDA Software to Go: Download Resources

There are a huge number of programs you can download that can make your PDA more fun and useful when you hit the road. Pocket PC or Palm OS, makes no difference. You can find a download that will make your PDA a much better travel companion.

We offer a few of our favorites here, but your best bet is to get on the Web before you leave and head to a download library. You can find a program that will make your PDA wake you up in the morning, find the best route to a meeting, tell you your bank balance, and pick up the bill for lunch. Well, maybe not that last one. But the others—definitely.

Where to Start: Download Libraries

Download.com   www.download.com   This CNET site offers all sorts of downloads for all sorts of computers. A good bet if you can't find what you're looking for anywhere else.

Tucows   www.tucows.com   Another general site, with tons of free (and inexpensive) downloads. You can find programs listed by PDA type, including RIM BlackBerry and EPOC-based handhelds.

Tucows writes its own reviews of software. If something gets five cows, it's a keeper. This site is highly recommended.

Palm   www.palm.com/software   A good place to start for Palm OS users. You can find language translators, world clocks, e-books, and hundreds of other applications for making better use of time on the road.

Microsoft   www.pocketpc.com   The Pocket PC site tends to focus on software for sale (most apps sell for about $20). You can learn to speak Italian, take a world map with you, or find the best route for travel on the Tube in London. You can also find the most recent version of ActiveSync, Microsoft's free program for synchronizing data on Windows CE and Pocket PC handhelds.

ZDNet   www.zdnet.com/files   ZDNet has one of the largest download libraries around. Files are rated using a five-star system, and users weigh in with their comments on programs from the library. Note that a free registration is now required.

In Your Palm: PQAs for PDAs

PQAs (or Palm Query Applications) are handy downloads that will allow you to get the information you need quickly over a wireless Internet connection. Here are a few that travelers should keep in mind.

Yodlee2Go 2.01   www.yodlee.com   Yodlee is a service that lets you view your online accounts (including bills, financial accounts, e-mail, and news) in one place. You log in to Yodlee once, instead of having to enter in your password for each site you want to access. The program is free. A version is also available for Pocket PC.

AirInfo Wireless   www.rovenet.com   If you need to know when your plane is taking off or when a friend is arriving, check out AirInfo Wireless. You can find the flight status for airports around the world.

Go.com   air.go.com   This free program offers wireless access to portal site Go.com. You can view ABC News, ESPN, and find horoscope, weather, finance, and other up-to-date information. Also includes a language translator.

AltaVista: Shopping.com Everywhere   www.shopping.com/everywhere
AltaVista's comparison-shopping site goes wireless. You can compare products and get detailed information before buying online. A version is also available for Pocket PC.

Put It in Your Pocket: Apps for Pocket PCs

MetrO 3.05   home.worldnet.fr or www.cearchives.com/travel.html   MetrO can quickly give you the fastest route between two subway stations in 115 cities worldwide. Whether you're in New York or Paris, you'll be set.

AvantGo   www.avantgo.com   We've talked about AvantGo quite a bit in the book. The service is a great way to download your choice of hundreds of Internet sites, including sports, weather, news, and stock info, when you synch up. No wireless modem? No problem. You can take the sites with you and browse them offline. If you do have a wireless modem, you can browse sites wirelessly from wherever you are. Here's the download that makes it happen. A version is also available for Palm OS handhelds.

pTravelAlarm 1.20   www.burroak.on.ca   Why carry around an extra alarm clock (or trust one you've never seen before)? If your Pocket PC goes on trips with you, install this travel alarm clock and make it pay its own way. You can choose from different alarms, and even set the length of time for the snooze button.

Traveller   www.twopeaks.com   This pocket itinerary tracker helps you stay on top of all your travel information, including where you stay, what you eat, where you go, and how you get there. You can store frequent flyer information, as well as your account numbers and passwords. A 30-day trial is available, which costs $19.95 to buy.

Index